Pillsbury

the big book of easy baking

with refrigerated dough

Houghton Mifflin Harcourt
Boston • New York • 2014

W9-BKJ-415

GENERAL MILLS

Creative Content and Publishing Director:
Elizabeth Nientimp

Food Content Marketing Manager:
Heather Reid Liebo

Senior Editor: Grace Wells

Kitchen Manager: Ann Stuart

Recipe Development and Testing:
Pillsbury Kitchens

Photography: General Mills Photography
Studios and Image Library

HOUGHTON MIFFLIN HARCOURT

Publisher: Natalie Chapman

Editorial Director: Cindy Kitchel

Executive Editor: Anne Ficklen

Editorial Assistant: Molly Aronica

Managing Editor: Marina Padakis

Production Editor: Jamie Selzer

Cover Design: Tai Blanche

Art Director and Book Design: Tai Blanche

Production Coordinator: Kimberly Kiefer

For information about permission to reproduce selections from this book, write to Permissions, Houghton Mifflin Harcourt Publishing Company, 215 Park Avenue South, New York, New York 10003.

www.hmhco.com

Library of Congress Cataloging-in-Publication Data:
The big book of easy baking with refrigerated dough.
     pages cm
At head of title: Pillsbury.
Includes index.
ISBN 978-0-544-33316-1 (paperback); 978-0-544-33342-0 (ebk)
1. Cooking (Frozen foods) 2. Frozen baked products. 3. Refrigerated foods.
4. Make-ahead cooking. I. Pillsbury Company. II. Title: Pillsbury the big book of easy baking with refrigerated dough.
TX828.B54 2014
641.6'153—dc23

                                   2014020818

Manufactured in the United States of America

DOC 10 9 8 7 6 5 4 3 2 1

Cover photo: Top (left to right): Thai Chicken Burgers (page 103); Gluten-Free Tomato and Mozzarella Pizza (page 148); Baked Sugar Doughnuts (page 256)

Bottom (left to right): Biscuit-Topped Vegetable Casserole (page 204); Gluten-Free Double Chocolate Sandwich Cookies (page 284)

For more great recipes visit
pillsbury.com

Dear Friends,

From traditional crescent rolls and biscuits to the newer gluten-free dough products, Pillsbury has always been there for you—helping make great meals and treats for your family to enjoy. That wonderful tradition continues with this collection of delicious recipes to choose from, all made with easy-to-use Pillsbury™ refrigerated dough.

In *The Big Book of Easy Baking*, you'll find an amazing array of recipes, all using one of the famous dough products, helping you turn refrigerated dough into a variety of family favorites. The selection includes foods for any time of the day from appetizers, sandwiches and hearty main dishes to wonderful desserts and cookies. Also, for those times when you just want a quick, really simple topping idea for biscuits or crescent rolls, see our special feature on page 8 for some fun ideas you'll want to try.

Be sure to check out a selection of Pillsbury Bake-Off© recipes too. It's fun to make recipes like Chicken-Bacon-Portabella Burgers, page 72, Roasted Vegetable Tart, page 202 or Sweet and Salty Cookie Pie, page 239, knowing that they were entered in this famous contest—and maybe won a prize!

So go ahead and pop the can to make and bake a delicious appetizer, main dish or treat everyone will love.

Delicious meals are at your fingertips. Let the making begin!

Sincerely,

Grace Wells
Pillsbury Editor

contents

make magic with pillsbury refrigerated dough

Since the 1951 introduction of refrigerated biscuits, the refrigerated dough revolution has moved ahead with a wonderful variety of products that simplify our baking. These products are amazing time-savers whether you are making a meal, snack or treat. Although each product is special in its own way, in general, they require no kneading or rolling and are very convenient and easy to use—just pop the can, make and bake!

- Over the years, Pillsbury has continued to meet the demand for innovative products and recipes, making our lives easier—favorites include biscuits, crescent rolls, pizza crust, pie crust and cookie dough. Plus, we now include gluten-free refrigerated dough in our product lineup. Look for recipes that use gluten-free pizza crust, gluten-free pie crust and gluten-free cookie dough.

- Nothing beats the aroma and taste of a freshly baked meal or treat from the oven, and with the ease of convenient dough products, it's an easy task. For the best results, here are some tips to guide you in the use of refrigerated dough products.

  - Store refrigerated dough on a shelf in the refrigerator. Temperatures in the crisper or on the door may be too cold or too warm. Also, keep dough refrigerated until you are ready to use it. After you open the can or package, use it right away because warm dough may be sticky and hard to handle.

  - For food safety reasons, any can of refrigerated dough left unrefrigerated for more than two hours should be thrown away.

  - Use refrigerated dough by the use-by date on the can or package. Most of the dough products should not be frozen as the dough may darken and will not rise during baking. Exceptions are pie crust and cookie dough—they can both be frozen for up to two months.

  - Always preheat the oven before baking with refrigerated dough. This will help prevent the dough from baking unevenly.

- Most recipes made with refrigerated dough are best warm from the oven, but they can easily be stored and reheated. Follow directions in the specific recipe for storage directions, but in general, most main dishes or anything that includes dairy products should be stored in the refrigerator.

Simple Pop-and-Tops for Biscuits

This cookbook includes an amazing variety of biscuit recipes to tempt you and your family. But sometimes it's nice to just pop the can and bake the biscuits. If you are looking for some simple flavor additions to add to biscuits, look no further — here you go!

Before baking them, top 8 bisquits with one of the following combinations after placing them on the cookie sheet. Then bake the biscuits as directed on the can.

- **Garlic Biscuits:** Mix 1 tablespoon olive oil or melted butter with ⅛ teaspoon garlic powder and brush on the biscuits.

- **Herb Biscuits:** Mix 1 tablespoon olive oil or melted butter with ½ teaspoon dried basil, oregano, crushed rosemary or Italian seasoning and brush on the biscuits.

- **Parmesan Biscuits:** Mix 1 tablespoon olive oil or melted butter with 1 to 2 tablespoons shredded Parmesan cheese and brush on the biscuits.

- **Cheesy Cheddar Biscuits:** Sprinkle biscuits with ¼ cup finely shredded Cheddar cheese and 2 teaspoons chopped fresh parsley.

- **Two-Seed Biscuits:** Brush biscuits with 1 tablespoon melted butter. Sprinkle with 1 teaspoon each poppy seed and sesame seed.

- **Cinnamon-Sugar Biscuits:** Brush biscuits with 1 tablespoon melted butter. Sprinkle with 1 tablespoon sugar and ⅛ to ¼ teaspoon ground cinnamon.

Creative Pop-and-Tops for Crescents

Great to use for making fabulous rolls, desserts and a huge variety of savory dishes, crescent rolls remain a favorite for any day of the week. But when you just want to bake them up, why not add a little pizzazz with a quick topping. Here are some suggestions — just pop the can, roll the crescents and add a quick topping to 8 crescent rolls.

- Before baking, brush with beaten whole egg or egg white and 1 to 2 tablespoons Italian dressing or milk. Bake as directed on the can.

- After baking, brush and sprinkle with one of the following combinations. Serve warm.

  - **Salty Crescents:** Brush with 1 tablespoon olive oil or melted butter. Sprinkle with 1 teaspoon coarse salt and ¼ teaspoon garlic powder.

  - **Taco Crescents:** Brush with 1 tablespoon olive oil or melted butter. Sprinkle with 1 tablespoon taco seasoning.

- **Herb Crescents:** Brush with 1 tablespoon olive oil or melted butter. Sprinkle with ½ to 1 teaspoon dried basil or oregano.

- **Cornbread Crescents:** Brush with 1 to 2 tablespoons honey or maple syrup. Sprinkle with 1 to 2 tablespoons yellow cornmeal.

- **Honey Crescents:** Brush with 1 to 2 tablespoons honey or maple syrup.

- **Cinnamon-Sugar Crescents:** Brush with 1 tablespoon melted butter. Sprinkle with 1 tablespoon sugar and ⅛ to ¼ teaspoon ground cinnamon.

Glazed Bacon Rollups (page 30)

appetizers

jalapeño-chicken crescent pinwheels

prep time: 20 Minutes • **start to finish:** 40 Minutes • 32 pinwheels

4 oz (half of 8-oz package) cream cheese, softened

½ cup chopped cooked chicken

¼ cup chopped fresh cilantro

2 to 3 tablespoons finely chopped sliced jalapeño chiles (from 12-oz jar)

⅛ teaspoon salt

2 medium green onions, finely chopped (2 tablespoons)

1 can (8 oz) Pillsbury refrigerated crescent dinner rolls (8 rolls)

1 Heat oven to 375°F. In small bowl, mix all ingredients except dough; set aside.

2 Unroll dough; separate into 2 long rectangles. Place 1 rectangle on cutting board; press perforations to seal. Spread half of cream cheese mixture on dough rectangle to within ½ inch of edges.

3 Starting with one long side, roll up rectangle; press seam to seal. With serrated knife, cut roll into 16 slices; place cut side down on ungreased cookie sheet. Repeat with remaining dough rectangle.

4 Bake 14 to 16 minutes or until light golden brown. Immediately remove from cookie sheet. Serve warm.

1 Pinwheel: Calories 45; Total Fat 3g (Saturated Fat 1.5g, Trans Fat 0g); Cholesterol 5mg; Sodium 85mg; Total Carbohydrate 3g (Dietary Fiber 0g); Protein 1g
Exchanges: 1 Fat **Carbohydrate Choices:** 0

buffalo chicken pinwheels

prep time: 20 Minutes • **start to finish:** 40 Minutes • 24 pinwheels

1 can (8 oz) Pillsbury refrigerated crescent dinner rolls (8 rolls) or 1 can (8 oz) Pillsbury™ Crescent Recipe Creations™ refrigerated seamless dough sheet

½ cup finely chopped cooked chicken

¾ teaspoon red pepper sauce

2 oz cream cheese, softened

¼ cup crumbled blue cheese (1 oz)

2 tablespoons chopped fresh chives

1 Heat oven to 350°F. Spray cookie sheet with cooking spray.

2 If using crescent rolls, unroll dough; separate into 4 rectangles. Press perforations to seal. If using dough sheet, unroll dough; cut into 4 rectangles.

3 In small bowl, mix chicken and pepper sauce until well coated. Spread 1 tablespoon cream cheese over each rectangle to within ¼ inch of edges. Sprinkle evenly with chicken mixture, blue cheese and chives.

4 Starting with one short side, roll up each rectangle; press edge to seal. With serrated knife, cut each roll into 6 slices; place cut side down on cookie sheet.

5 Bake 13 to 17 minutes or until edges are golden brown. Serve warm.

1 Pinwheel: Calories 50; Total Fat 3.5g (Saturated Fat 1.5g, Trans Fat 0.5g); Cholesterol 5mg; Sodium 100mg; Total Carbohydrate 4g (Dietary Fiber 0g); Protein 2g
Exchanges: ½ High-Fat Meat **Carbohydrate Choices:** 0

Easy Success Tips

Prepare and bake these appetizers up to 24 hours ahead of time, then cover and refrigerate. Before serving, place the appetizers in a shallow pan, and cover with foil. Heat at 350°F for 10 to 15 minutes or until hot.

Add to the Buffalo flavors by serving the pinwheels with blue cheese dip and celery sticks.

three-cheese pinwheels

prep time: **15 Minutes** • start to finish: **35 Minutes** • **16 pinwheels**

½ **cup crumbled blue cheese (2 oz)**

¼ **cup shredded pepper Jack cheese (1 oz)**

2 **tablespoons cream cheese, softened**

1 **tablespoon mayonnaise or salad dressing**

1 **can Pillsbury™ Place 'n Bake™ refrigerated crescent rounds (8 rounds)**

2 **teaspoons chopped fresh parsley**

1 Heat oven to 375°F. Lightly spray cookie sheet with cooking spray. In small bowl, mix cheeses and mayonnaise until well blended and soft.

2 Unroll dough on work surface. Spread cheese mixture evenly over dough. Starting with one short side, roll up rectangle; pinch edges to seal. Cut roll into 16 slices. Place cut side down on cookie sheet. Sprinkle with parsley.

3 Bake 12 to 15 minutes or until golden brown. Immediately remove from cookie sheet; cool 3 minutes. Serve warm.

1 Pinwheel: Calories 80; Total Fat 6g (Saturated Fat 2.5g, Trans Fat 1g); Cholesterol 5mg; Sodium 180mg; Total Carbohydrate 6g (Dietary Fiber 0g); Protein 2g **Exchanges:** ½ Starch, 1 Fat **Carbohydrate Choices:** ½

Easy Success Tip

If you're trying to tempt tiny taste buds, steer clear of French Roquefort, and choose a milder blue cheese such as Danablu, Gorgonzola, Stilton or Maytag Blue.

upside-down tomato, basil and chicken tartlets

prep time: 30 Minutes • **start to finish:** 55 Minutes • 8 tartlets

⅓ cup extra-virgin olive oil

4½ teaspoons crushed red pepper and garlic seasoning blend

½ cup finely chopped deli rotisserie chicken breast

3 sticks (1 oz each) mozzarella string cheese or tomato basil string cheese, finely chopped

8 thin plum (Roma) tomato slices (1 medium)

¼ teaspoon salt

1 can Pillsbury Place 'n Bake refrigerated crescent rounds (8 rounds)

1 tablespoon finely chopped fresh basil leaves

1 Heat oven to 375°F. In small bowl, mix oil and 2 teaspoons of the seasoning blend. Let stand 5 minutes to blend flavors. In another small bowl, mix chicken, cheese and 2 teaspoons of the seasoning blend. Generously grease 8 nonstick regular-size muffin cups with 2 teaspoons of the olive oil mixture.

2 Blot excess liquid from tomato slices with paper towels. Sprinkle with salt and ¼ teaspoon of the seasoning blend. Place one tomato slice, seasoned side down, in bottom of each muffin cup.

3 Remove dough from can, but do not separate. With serrated knife, cut dough evenly into 16 rounds. Press each into 3-inch round. Sprinkle remaining ¼ teaspoon seasoning blend over 8 of the rounds.

4 Press seasoned rounds, seasoned side down, over tomato slices and partially up sides of muffin cups. Evenly divide chicken mixture into each cup. Top each with 1 of remaining crescent rounds. Press rounds so tops are even and tartlets will sit flat when removed from muffin cups.

5 Bake 13 to 16 minutes or until deep golden brown. Let stand 5 minutes. Run knife around edges to loosen. Turn muffin pan upside down onto heatproof platter to remove tartlets. Sprinkle with basil. Drizzle with remaining oil mixture or use for dipping.

1 Tartlet: Calories 230; Total Fat 18g (Saturated Fat 4.5g, Trans Fat 1.5g); Cholesterol 15mg; Sodium 570mg; Total Carbohydrate 12g (Dietary Fiber 0g); Protein 7g
Exchanges: 1 Starch, ½ Lean Meat, 3 Fat **Carbohydrate Choices:** 1

sweet chili chicken sliders

prep time: 30 Minutes • **start to finish:** 30 Minutes • 10 servings

- 1 can (12 oz) Pillsbury™ Grands!™ Jr. Golden Layers™ Butter Tastin'™ refrigerated biscuits (10 biscuits)
- 1 lb ground chicken
- ⅔ cup sweet chili sauce
- ½ teaspoon salt
- ¼ teaspoon pepper
- ½ cup peach-apricot preserves
- 1 cup mayonnaise with olive oil or mayonnaise
- 2 tablespoons Sriracha sauce
- 2 cups coleslaw mix (shredded cabbage and carrots), coarsely chopped

1 Heat oven to 400°F. Bake biscuits as directed on can.

2 Meanwhile, in medium bowl, mix chicken, 2 tablespoons of the chili sauce, the salt and pepper. Shape chicken mixture into 10 (½-inch thick) patties. In 12-inch nonstick skillet, cook patties over medium-high heat 6 to 9 minutes, turning once, until meat thermometer inserted in center of chicken patties reads at least 165°F. During the last few minutes of cooking, brush chicken patties with remaining chili sauce.

3 Place preserves, mayonnaise and Sriracha sauce in food processor. Cover; process 10 to 15 seconds or until smooth.

4 In medium bowl, mix ½ cup of the preserves mixture and the coleslaw mix; toss to coat.

5 Split biscuits. Top bottom of each biscuit with chicken patty, coleslaw mixture and top half of biscuit. Serve warm with remaining preserves mixture.

1 Serving: Calories 340; Total Fat 17g (Saturated Fat 3.5g, Trans Fat 2g); Cholesterol 35mg; Sodium 950mg; Total Carbohydrate 37g (Dietary Fiber 1g); Protein 8g **Exchanges:** 2½ Starch, 3 Fat **Carbohydrate Choices:** 2½

turkey and cherry sandwich minis

prep time: 20 Minutes • **start to finish:** 45 Minutes • **16 sandwiches**

1 can Pillsbury™ refrigerated crusty French loaf

2 slices bacon, finely chopped

3 tablespoons mayonnaise

¼ cup crumbled blue cheese (1 oz)

¼ cup cherry preserves

8 oz thinly sliced deli smoked turkey breast

4 large red lettuce leaves, cut into quarters

1 Heat oven to 350°F. Spray large cookie sheet with cooking spray.

2 Place dough on work surface. Flatten loaf of dough to 18 inches long and 2 inches thick. Cut in half lengthwise. With serrated knife, cut each half into 8 slices to make 16 buns. Place on cookie sheet. Bake 17 to 20 minutes or until golden brown. Remove to cooling rack; cool 10 minutes.

3 Meanwhile, in 8-inch nonstick skillet, cook bacon over medium-high heat 3 to 5 minutes, stirring occasionally, until crisp. Drain on paper towel. In small bowl, mix bacon, mayonnaise and blue cheese.

4 Cut each mini bun in half horizontally to within ¼ inch of other side; open each bun to lie flat. Spread about 1 teaspoon mayonnaise mixture on bottom half of each bun. Spread about ½ teaspoon preserves on top half of each bun. Fill sandwiches with turkey slices and lettuce. Fold tops over lettuce.

1 Sandwich: Calories 110; Total Fat 4g (Saturated Fat 1g, Trans Fat 0g); Cholesterol 10mg; Sodium 340mg; Total Carbohydrate 13g (Dietary Fiber 0g); Protein 4g **Exchanges:** ½ Starch, ½ Other Carbohydrate, ½ Very Lean Meat, ½ Fat **Carbohydrate Choices:** 1

brussels sprouts and bacon crescent cups

prep time: 25 Minutes • **start to finish:** 45 Minutes • **16 appetizers**

1 box (10 oz) frozen baby Brussels sprouts and butter sauce

1 teaspoon canola oil

¼ cup finely chopped red onion

1 can (8 oz) Pillsbury refrigerated crescent dinner rolls (8 rolls)

8 slices packaged precooked bacon, cut in half

½ cup shredded pepper Jack cheese (2 oz)

1 Heat oven to 350°F. Spray 16 regular-size muffin cups with cooking spray, or line large cookie sheet with cooking parchment paper. Microwave frozen Brussels sprouts as directed on box; set aside to cool slightly.

2 Meanwhile, in 8-inch skillet, heat oil over medium-high heat. Add onion; cook 2 minutes, stirring occasionally, until soft. Set aside.

3 Remove dough from package, but do not unroll. Using serrated knife, cut evenly into 16 rounds; carefully separate rounds. Shape each round into a ball; flatten to 2½-inch round. Spoon about ¼ teaspoon of the onion in center of each round. Wrap ½ bacon strip around each Brussels sprout; place on onion, Brussels sprout side up. Bring edge of dough up sides of each bacon-wrapped Brussels sprout to form a cup, pressing dough firmly to secure. Place in muffin cups. Top each with heaping teaspoon cheese; press in lightly. Drizzle any remaining butter sauce over cups.

4 Bake 12 to 17 minutes or until edges are golden brown. Serve warm.

1 Appetizer: Calories 100; Total Fat 6g (Saturated Fat 2.5g, Trans Fat 1g); Cholesterol 10mg; Sodium 280mg; Total Carbohydrate 7g (Dietary Fiber 0g); Protein 3g **Exchanges:** ½ Starch, 1 Fat **Carbohydrate Choices:** ½

Easy Success Tip

You will need 16 Brussels sprouts for this recipe. Cut larger ones in half, if needed.

grands! chicken thai-spiced cups

prep time: 15 Minutes • **start to finish:** 35 Minutes • 20 appetizers

1 cup finely chopped cooked chicken

¼ cup finely chopped cilantro or green onions (4 medium)

¼ cup finely chopped red bell pepper

¼ cup Thai peanut sauce

1 can (10.2 oz) Pillsbury™ Grands!™ Flaky Layers or Homestyle refrigerated buttermilk or original biscuits (5 biscuits)

1 Heat oven to 375°F. Spray 20 mini muffin cups with cooking spray.

2 In medium bowl, mix chicken, 3 tablespoons of the cilantro, the bell pepper and peanut sauce; set aside.

3 Separate dough into 5 biscuits. Cut each biscuit into quarters. Flatten each dough piece. Place 1 piece in each muffin cup; firmly press in bottom and up side of cup.

4 Spoon and press about 2 teaspoons chicken mixture into each dough-lined cup.

5 Bake 12 to 16 minutes or until golden brown. Remove from muffin cups. Sprinkle with remaining cilantro. Serve warm.

1 Appetizer: Calories 70; Total Fat 3g (Saturated Fat 1g, Trans Fat 0.5g); Cholesterol 5mg; Sodium 150mg; Total Carbohydrate 7g (Dietary Fiber 0g); Protein 3g **Exchanges:** ½ Starch, ½ Fat **Carbohydrate Choices:** ½

Easy Success Tip

If you prefer to make these cups with green onions instead of cilantro, garnish the tops with additional onions before serving.

chipotle meatball appetizers

prep time: 30 Minutes • **start to finish:** 50 Minutes • **24 appetizers**

1 can (8 oz) Pillsbury refrigerated crescent dinner rolls (8 rolls)

1 tablespoon vegetable oil

½ cup finely chopped onion

1 chipotle chile in adobo sauce, finely chopped, plus 3 tablespoons adobo sauce (from 7-oz can)

12 frozen Italian-style meatballs (½ oz each), thawed, halved

2 tablespoons water

4 pieces mozzarella string cheese (1 oz each)

1 medium avocado, pitted, peeled and cut into 24 small slices

1 Heat oven to 350°F. Spray 24 mini muffin cups with cooking spray. Separate dough into 4 rectangles; press perforations to seal. Cut each rectangle into 6 squares. Press each square in bottom and up side of mini muffin cup. Bake 6 minutes. Remove from oven. Using handle of wooden spoon, immediately make 1½-inch indentation in center of each cup.

2 Meanwhile, in 10-inch skillet, heat oil over medium heat. Add onion; cook 2 to 3 minutes or until tender. Stir in chipotle chile and adobo sauce, meatballs and water. Cover; reduce heat to low. Cook 3 to 4 minutes, stirring occasionally, until thoroughly heated. Remove meatballs from skillet. Spoon ½ teaspoon of the sauce into each cup. Top each with 1 meatball half, cut side up.

3 Cut each piece string cheese lengthwise in half; cut each half crosswise into thirds. Top each meatball with 1 piece string cheese. Bake 6 to 10 minutes longer or until edges are golden brown. Cool 1 minute; remove from muffin cups.

4 Top each meatball cup with 1 avocado slice; secure with wooden toothpick. Serve warm.

1 Appetizer: Calories 90; Total Fat 6g (Saturated Fat 2g, Trans Fat 0g); Cholesterol 5mg; Sodium 150mg; Total Carbohydrate 5g (Dietary Fiber 0g); Protein 3g **Exchanges:** ½ Other Carbohydrate, ½ High-Fat Meat, ½ Fat **Carbohydrate Choices:** ½

grands! spinach and feta foldovers

prep time: **25 Minutes** • start to finish: **50 Minutes** • **16 appetizers**

1 package (4 oz) crumbled feta cheese (1 cup)

1 box (9 oz) frozen chopped spinach, thawed, squeezed to drain

3 medium green onions, chopped (3 tablespoons)

½ teaspoon finely shredded lemon peel

¼ teaspoon salt

⅛ teaspoon pepper

1 can (16.3 oz) Pillsbury Grands! Homestyle refrigerated buttermilk or original biscuits (8 biscuits)

Tzatziki or cucumber-yogurt sauce, if desired

1 Heat oven to 375°F. Spray large cookie sheet with cooking spray.

2 In medium bowl, place feta cheese; break apart large pieces with fork. Add spinach, onions, lemon peel, salt and pepper; mix well.

3 Separate dough into 8 biscuits. Separate each biscuit into 2 layers. Press or roll each to form 3½-inch round. Spoon about 2 tablespoons spinach mixture in center of each round. Fold dough over filling, pressing firmly to compress filling; firmly press edges of dough with fork to seal. Place on cookie sheet.

4 Bake 12 to 16 minutes or until golden brown. Cool 5 minutes. Serve warm with tzatziki sauce.

1 Appetizer: Calories 120; Total Fat 6g (Saturated Fat 2.5g, Trans Fat 1g); Cholesterol 10mg; Sodium 420mg; Total Carbohydrate 13g (Dietary Fiber 0g); Protein 3g **Exchanges:** 1 Starch, 1 Fat **Carbohydrate Choices:** 1

Easy Success Tip

Tzatziki sauce and cucumber-yogurt sauce are traditional Greek yogurt sauces made with cucumbers and herbs. Look for them in the refrigerated section of the deli area at your grocery store.

chorizo party appetizers

prep time: 25 Minutes • **start to finish:** 25 Minutes • 8 appetizers

1 can Pillsbury Place
'n Bake refrigerated
crescent rounds
(8 rounds)

½ lb Mexican chorizo pork
sausage links or bulk
sausage

¼ cup canola oil

½ peeled mango, cut into
8 thin slices

2 oz Gouda cheese,
shredded (½ cup)

1 tablespoon finely
chopped seeded
jalapeño chile

2 tablespoons finely
chopped roasted red bell
pepper (from a jar)

1 Heat oven to 375°F. Bake crescent rounds as directed on can. Remove from oven. Immediately press back of soup spoon in center of each round to make an indentation. Reduce oven temperature to 300°F.

2 Meanwhile, remove casings from sausage. In 10-inch nonstick skillet, break up sausage; cook over medium heat 8 to 10 minutes, stirring occasionally, until thoroughly cooked. Drain. Set aside.

3 In 8-inch skillet, heat oil over medium-high heat. Add mango slices; cook 1 to 2 minutes on each side or until hot. Drain on paper towels.

4 Fill each baked crescent round with 1 heaping tablespoon sausage; press in lightly. Top with cheese and mango. Bake 5 to 6 minutes longer or until cheese is melted.

5 Meanwhile, in small bowl, mix chile and roasted pepper. Sprinkle chile mixture over appetizers. Serve warm.

1 Appetizer: Calories 230; Total Fat 16g (Saturated Fat 5g, Trans Fat 1.5g); Cholesterol 20mg; Sodium 380mg; Total Carbohydrate 15g (Dietary Fiber 0g); Protein 6g **Exchanges:** 1 Starch, ½ Medium-Fat Meat, 2½ Fat **Carbohydrate Choices:** 1

grands! cranberry-glazed meatball appetizers

prep time: **25 Minutes** • start to finish: **50 Minutes** • **16 appetizers**

8 frozen meatballs, thawed, chopped

⅓ cup chili sauce

¼ cup jellied cranberry sauce (from 14-oz can)

1 can (16.3 oz) Pillsbury Grands! Flaky Layers refrigerated buttermilk or original biscuits (8 biscuits)

1 egg, beaten

1 Heat oven to 350°F. Spray cookie sheet with cooking spray.

2 In medium bowl, mix meatballs, chili sauce and cranberry sauce.

3 Separate dough into 8 biscuits. Separate each biscuit into 2 layers. Press or roll each to form 4-inch round. Spoon about 1 tablespoon meatball mixture onto center of each dough round. Wrap dough around meatball mixture; bring up edge of dough, pinching together tightly to form bundle. Place on cookie sheet; brush with egg.

4 Bake 18 to 22 minutes or until golden brown. Serve warm.

1 Appetizer: Calories 140; Total Fat 6g (Saturated Fat 1.5g, Trans Fat 1g); Cholesterol 25mg; Sodium 430mg; Total Carbohydrate 17g (Dietary Fiber 0g); Protein 4g **Exchanges:** 1 Starch, 1 Fat **Carbohydrate Choices:** 1

Easy Success Tip

The dough needs to be pinched very firmly so the filling does not cook out.

glazed bacon rollups

prep time: 15 Minutes • **start to finish:** 30 Minutes • 12 rollups

¼ cup Concord grape jelly

¾ cup packed brown sugar

2 tablespoons Dijon mustard

1 can Pillsbury™ refrigerated original breadsticks

12 slices packaged precooked bacon

2 tablespoons thinly sliced green onion tops (3 medium)

1 Heat oven to 375°F. Lightly spray 12 regular-size muffin cups and top of pan with cooking spray.

2 In 2-cup microwavable measuring cup, stir jelly, brown sugar and mustard until well blended. Microwave uncovered on High 1 minute. Stir until smooth. Microwave 15 seconds longer or until syrupy. Pour into shallow microwavable dish.

3 Unroll dough; carefully separate into 12 breadsticks. Press breadsticks to length of bacon slices. For each rollup, dip 1 bacon slice into syrup mixture, turning to coat both sides; shake off excess. Place on breadstick. Starting at one short end, roll up; place in muffin cup, flat side up. Repeat with remaining breadsticks and bacon slices. If syrup mixture thickens, microwave on High 10 seconds; stir.

4 Bake 10 to 13 minutes or until rollups are puffed and light golden brown. Turn muffin pan upside down onto heatproof platter, allowing syrup to drip down sides of rollups. Sprinkle with green onions. Serve warm.

1 Rollup: Calories 190; Total Fat 5g (Saturated Fat 2g, Trans Fat 0g); Cholesterol 10mg; Sodium 430mg; Total Carbohydrate 31g (Dietary Fiber 0g); Protein 5g **Exchanges:** 2 Starch, 1 Fat **Carbohydrate Choices:** 2

salted beer pretzel crescents

prep time: **10 Minutes** • start to finish: **25 Minutes** • **8 appetizers**

1 can (8 oz) Pillsbury refrigerated crescent dinner rolls (8 rolls)

½ cup shredded Cheddar cheese (2 oz)

1 egg

1 bottle (12 oz) stout beer

¼ cup baking soda

1 teaspoon coarse (kosher or sea) salt

1 Heat oven to 375°F. Spray cookie sheet with cooking spray or line with cooking parchment paper.

2 Separate dough into 8 triangles. Place 1 tablespoon cheese on wide end of each triangle. Starting with short side, roll up to opposite point.

3 In small bowl, beat egg and 1 tablespoon of the beer with whisk until blended; set aside.

4 In large microwavable bowl, microwave remaining beer uncovered on High 1 minute 30 seconds or until hot. Slowly add baking soda; stir until dissolved. Dip each crescent, one at a time, into beer mixture. Remove with large pancake turner or slotted spoon; place on cooling rack. Let stand at room temperature about 5 minutes.

5 Brush crescents with egg mixture, and sprinkle with salt. Carefully transfer to cookie sheet. Curve ends of each into crescent shape. Bake 10 to 12 minutes or until tops are deep golden brown. Serve warm.

1 Appetizer: Calories 140; Total Fat 9g (Saturated Fat 4g, Trans Fat 0g); Cholesterol 30mg; Sodium 1040mg; Total Carbohydrate 12g; (Dietary Fiber 0g); Protein 3g. **Exchanges:** 1 starch, 1½ Fat **Carbohydrate Choices:** 1

gluten-free bacon-cheese squares

prep time: 20 Minutes • **start to finish:** 40 Minutes • **50 appetizers**

1 container Pillsbury™ Gluten Free refrigerated pie and pastry dough

1 container (8 oz) gluten-free chive and onion cream cheese spread

⅓ cup gluten-free cooked real bacon pieces (from 3-oz package)

25 grape tomatoes, cut in half

½ cup chopped green onions (8 medium)

1 Heat oven to 425°F. Divide dough in half. Knead each half until softened and no longer crumbly. Flatten each into a round.

2 Place 1 round between 2 sheets of cooking parchment or waxed paper. Roll into 10-inch square. Carefully peel off top sheet of paper. With pizza cutter or knife, cut dough into 25 (2-inch) squares. Replace paper; carefully turn dough over, and remove second sheet of paper. Place squares on ungreased cookie sheet. Repeat with remaining dough.

3 Bake 8 to 11 minutes or until golden brown on edges. Cool 10 minutes.

4 Meanwhile, in small bowl, mix cream cheese spread and bacon. Top each pastry square with about 1 teaspoon cream cheese mixture. Top each with tomato half; sprinkle with green onions. Serve warm.

1 Appetizer: Calories 100; Total Fat 7g (Saturated Fat 2.5g, Trans Fat 0g); Cholesterol 0mg; Sodium 140mg; Total Carbohydrate 8g (Dietary Fiber 0g); Protein 0g **Exchanges:** ½ Other Carbohydrate, 1½ Fat **Carbohydrate Choices:** ½

Easy Success Tips

Top these gluten-free squares with other toppings, such as hummus or refried beans. Sprinkle with chopped olives or cilantro leaves.

If you are cooking gluten free, always read labels to make sure each recipe ingredient is gluten free. Products and ingredient sources can change.

gluten-free greek appetizer pizza

prep time: 10 Minutes • **start to finish:** 35 Minutes • **20 appetizers**

- 1 container Pillsbury™ Gluten Free refrigerated pizza crust dough
- 1 cup shredded mozzarella cheese (4 oz)
- 1 jar (6 oz) marinated artichoke hearts, drained, coarsely chopped
- ⅓ cup drained pitted kalamata olives, cut in half
- ⅓ cup roasted red bell peppers (from a jar), drained, chopped
- 2 oz gluten-free crumbled tomato and basil feta cheese (½ cup)

1 Heat oven to 400°F. Grease cookie sheet and hands. Press dough into 12x10-inch rectangle on cookie sheet.

2 Bake 10 to 12 minutes or until edges are beginning to brown. Sprinkle with remaining ingredients.

3 Bake 6 to 9 minutes longer or until crust is deep golden brown and cheese is melted. Cut into 5 rows by 4 rows. Serve warm.

1 Appetizer: Calories 45; Total Fat 2.5g (Saturated Fat 1g, Trans Fat 0g); Cholesterol 5mg; Sodium 140mg; Total Carbohydrate 3g (Dietary Fiber 0g); Protein 2g **Exchanges:** ½ Medium-Fat Meat **Carbohydrate Choices:** 0

Easy Success Tips

You can substitute gluten-free herb and garlic feta or plain feta for the tomato and basil feta. If using plain feta, sprinkle about ½ teaspoon gluten-free Italian seasoning or basil over toppings before baking.

If you are cooking gluten free, always read labels to make sure each recipe ingredient is gluten free. Products and ingredient sources can change.

greek appetizer flatbread

prep time: 15 Minutes • **start to finish:** 15 Minutes • 6 servings (4 pieces each)

1 can Pillsbury™ refrigerated artisan pizza crust with whole grain

2 teaspoons Greek seasoning or dried oregano leaves

3 oz fat-free cream cheese, softened (from 8-oz package)

1 cup baby spinach leaves

½ cup thinly sliced red onion

⅓ cup pitted kalamata olives, cut in half

6 cherry tomatoes, cut into quarters

1 Heat oven to 400°F for dark or nonstick pan (425°F for all other pans). Spray 15x10x1-inch pan with cooking spray.

2 Unroll dough in pan; starting at center, press dough into 15x10-inch rectangle.

3 Bake 13 to 18 minutes or until edges of crust are golden brown.

4 In small bowl, stir Greek seasoning into cream cheese; spread over crust. Top with spinach, onion and olives. Serve immediately, or cover and refrigerate 1 to 2 hours before serving. To serve, cut into 6 rows by 4 rows. Top each piece with tomato.

1 Serving: Calories 220; Total Fat 6g (Saturated Fat 1g, Trans Fat 0g); Cholesterol 0mg; Sodium 530mg; Total Carbohydrate 33g (Dietary Fiber 2g); Protein 8g **Exchanges:** 2 Starch, ½ Vegetable, 1 Fat **Carbohydrate Choices:** 2

Easy Success Tips

For fresh flavor, top with ½ cup chopped cucumber.

Greek seasoning is a blend of oregano, onion powder and parsley. Look for it in the spice section of the supermarket.

asiago-crusted potato piroshki

prep time: 30 Minutes • **start to finish:** 50 Minutes • 20 appetizers

1 bag (11.8 oz) frozen seasoned backyard grilled potatoes

2 tablespoons olive oil

2 tablespoons butter

2 cups cleaned thinly sliced fresh leeks, white and light green portions only

½ to 1 teaspoon dried thyme leaves

2 cans (12 oz each) Pillsbury Grands! Jr. Golden Layers Butter Tastin' refrigerated biscuits (20 biscuits total)

1½ cups shredded Asiago cheese (6 oz)

1 Heat oven to 375°F. Line large cookie sheets with foil; spray with cooking spray. Microwave frozen potatoes as directed on bag.

2 Meanwhile, in 12-inch skillet, heat oil and butter over medium heat. Add leeks; cook 2 minutes, stirring occasionally. Add potatoes and thyme; cook 1 to 2 minutes longer, coarsely mashing potatoes with fork. Remove from heat; cool mixture slightly.

3 Separate cans of dough into 20 biscuits. Press each biscuit into 3½-inch round. Spoon about 1 heaping tablespoon potato filling in center of each round. Fold dough over filling; press edges to seal.

4 Place cheese in shallow dish. Press biscuits into cheese to generously coat all sides. Place 2 inches apart on cookie sheets.

5 Bake 11 to 15 minutes or until golden brown. Cool 2 minutes on cookie sheets. Serve warm.

1 Appetizer: Calories 190; Total Fat 10g (Saturated Fat 4.5g, Trans Fat 0g); Cholesterol 10mg; Sodium 520mg; Total Carbohydrate 19g (Dietary Fiber 0g); Protein 4g **Exchanges:** 1 Starch, ½ Vegetable, 2 Fat **Carbohydrate Choices:** 1

Easy Success Tip

Piroshki are small delicious Russian turnovers. They are served as appetizers and can be filled with savory or sweet fillings.

chile and cheese empanaditas

prep time: 25 Minutes • **start to finish:** 45 Minutes • 16 appetizers

1 cup shredded pepper Jack cheese (4 oz)

⅓ cup chopped green chiles (from 4.5-oz can)

1 box Pillsbury™ refrigerated pie crusts, softened as directed on box

1 egg, beaten

1 cup chunky-style salsa

1 Heat oven to 400°F. In small bowl, mix cheese and chiles.

2 With 3¼-inch round cutter, cut each pie crust into 8 rounds. Spoon cheese mixture evenly onto half of each dough round. Brush edge of each round with egg. Fold rounds in half; press edges with fork to seal. Place on ungreased cookie sheet. Brush tops of rounds with egg. Cut small slit in top of each.

3 Bake 12 to 16 minutes or until golden brown. Serve warm with salsa.

1 Appetizer: Calories 120; Total Fat 7g (Saturated Fat 3.5g, Trans Fat 0g); Cholesterol 20mg; Sodium 300mg; Total Carbohydrate 12g (Dietary Fiber 0g); Protein 2g
Exchanges: 1 Starch, 1 Fat **Carbohydrate Choices:** 1

Easy Success Tips

No pepper Jack cheese? Use Cheddar cheese instead.

Empanar is Spanish for "to bake in pastry." These bite-size pastry snacks are the perfect lead-in to a Mexican meal.

gluten-free spinach mini quiches

prep time: 30 Minutes • **start to finish:** 1 Hour • 24 quiches

½ **container Pillsbury Gluten Free refrigerated pie and pastry dough**

2 **eggs**

½ **cup half-and-half**

⅓ **cup grated Parmesan cheese**

½ **teaspoon garlic salt**

¼ **teaspoon pepper**

1 **box (9 oz) frozen chopped spinach, thawed, squeezed to drain**

3 **tablespoons chopped green onions (3 medium)**

1 Heat oven to 425°F. Knead dough until softened and no longer crumbly. Press 1 rounded teaspoonful dough in bottom and up side of each of 24 ungreased mini muffin cups, extending dough ¼ inch above edge of each cup.

2 In medium bowl, beat eggs. Stir in half-and-half, cheese, garlic salt and pepper. Stir in spinach and green onions. Spoon about 1 tablespoonful mixture into each crust-lined cup.

3 Bake 16 to 18 minutes or until puffed and golden brown. Cool 5 minutes. Carefully remove from pan to cooling rack. Serve warm or cool. Store covered in refrigerator.

1 Quiche: Calories 100; Total Fat 7g (Saturated Fat 3g, Trans Fat 0g); Cholesterol 20mg; Sodium 170mg; Total Carbohydrate 8g (Dietary Fiber 0g); Protein 1g **Exchanges:** ½ Starch, 1½ Fat **Carbohydrate Choices:** ½

Easy Success Tips

Quiches are best when served warm. But you can save time by preparing the dough and filling separately ahead of time. Press dough into muffin cups; cover tightly, and refrigerate up to 24 hours. Mix filling ingredients; cover and refrigerate up to 24 hours. Bake and cool as directed.

If you are cooking gluten free, always read labels to make sure each recipe ingredient is gluten free. Products and ingredient sources can change.

mini tuscan vegetable wraps

prep time: 30 Minutes • **start to finish:** 45 Minutes • 18 servings

1 box (7 oz) frozen antioxidant blend broccoli, carrots and sweet peppers

2 tablespoons basil pesto

2 oz thinly sliced prosciutto (about 5 slices)

1 can (8 oz) Pillsbury Crescent Recipe Creations refrigerated seamless dough sheet

⅔ cup peach-apricot preserves

2 tablespoons spicy brown mustard

1 tablespoon finely chopped fresh basil leaves

1 Heat oven to 375°F. Microwave frozen vegetables as directed on box; cool 2 minutes. Finely chop vegetables. In medium bowl, mix vegetables and pesto; set aside. Cut prosciutto into thin strips.

2 Unroll dough sheet. Cut into 18 squares. In center of each square, spoon about 2 teaspoons vegetable mixture. Top each with prosciutto. Pull 2 opposite corners of dough over filling; pinch to seal. Place 1 inch apart on ungreased cookie sheet. Bake 10 to 15 minutes or until golden brown.

3 Meanwhile, in small bowl, mix preserves, mustard and basil. Serve with warm wraps. Garnish with additional basil sprigs, if desired.

1 Serving: Calories 90; Total Fat 3.5g (Saturated Fat 1g, Trans Fat 0g); Cholesterol 0mg; Sodium 190mg; Total Carbohydrate 14g (Dietary Fiber 0g); Protein 1g **Exchanges:** ½ Starch, ½ Other Carbohydrate, ½ Fat **Carbohydrate Choices:** 1

kickin' spinach-cheese bites

prep time: 30 Minutes • **start to finish:** 45 Minutes • 48 appetizers

1 box (9 oz) frozen chopped spinach

1 package (8 oz) cream cheese, softened

¼ cup ricotta cheese

6 oz provolone cheese, shredded (1½ cups)

¼ cup finely chopped pickled jalapeño slices, drained (from 11.5-oz jar)

2 cans Pillsbury Crescent Recipe Creations refrigerated seamless dough sheet

1 Heat oven to 375°F. Lightly spray 48 nonstick mini muffin cups with cooking spray. Microwave frozen spinach as directed on box. Squeeze dry with paper towels.

2 In medium bowl, beat cream cheese and ricotta cheese with electric mixer on medium speed until well blended. Stir in spinach, provolone cheese and jalapeño slices until well blended.

3 Unroll 1 dough sheet; press into 12x8-inch rectangle. Cut into 24 squares. Press 1 square in bottom and up side of each mini muffin cup. Spoon 1 rounded teaspoon spinach mixture into each cup. Repeat with remaining dough sheet and filling.

4 Bake 8 to 12 minutes or until edges of dough are golden brown. Immediately remove from muffin cups to serving platter. Cool 5 minutes. Serve warm.

1 Appetizer: Calories 60; Total Fat 4g (Saturated Fat 2g, Trans Fat 0g); Cholesterol 10mg; Sodium 135mg; Total Carbohydrate 5g (Dietary Fiber 0g); Protein 2g **Exchanges:** ½ Starch, ½ Fat **Carbohydrate Choices:** ½

grands! cheesy herb monkey bread

prep time: 15 Minutes • start to finish: 55 Minutes • 40 appetizers

⅓ cup butter, melted

¾ teaspoon dried dill weed

¾ teaspoon garlic powder

2 cans (10.2 oz each) Pillsbury Grands! Flaky Layers refrigerated buttermilk or original biscuits (10 biscuits total)

2½ cups shredded Colby–Monterey Jack cheese blend (10 oz)

1 Heat oven to 350°F. Generously grease 12-cup fluted tube cake pan with shortening, or spray with cooking spray.

2 In small bowl, mix melted butter, dill weed and garlic powder. Separate each can of dough into 5 biscuits; cut each biscuit into quarters. Coat half of the biscuit pieces in butter mixture; arrange in pan.

3 Sprinkle 2 cups of the cheese over dough. Coat remaining dough pieces in butter mixture; arrange over cheese. Sprinkle with remaining ½ cup cheese.

4 Bake 30 to 35 minutes or until golden brown. Let stand 5 minutes. Run knife around outside edge to loosen. Place heatproof plate upside down over pan; turn plate and pan over. Remove pan; turn upside down onto serving plate. Pull apart to serve.

1 Appetizer: Calories 90; Total Fat 6g (Saturated Fat 3g, Trans Fat 0.5g); Cholesterol 10mg; Sodium 180mg; Total Carbohydrate 6g (Dietary Fiber 0g); Protein 2g **Exchanges:** ½ Starch, 1 Fat **Carbohydrate Choices:** ½

Easy Success Tip

A pizza cutter works great to cut the biscuits into quarters super-fast!

Spotted Crescent Dogs

Your step-by-step guide to making the most adorable crescent dogs ever!

1: Prepare the Dough

Unroll 1 container of crescent dough on your work surface. Divide the dough into 4 rectangles (each rectangle will make 1 crescent dog); pinch the diagonal perforations to seal. Cut each rectangle in half crosswise. Cut one half of each rectangle into 6 thin strips.

2: Make the Body

Wrap the uncut half of each rectangle around a hot dog; pinch the seam to seal. Place seam side down on cookie sheet.

3: Make the Paws and Tail

For each dog, fold four of the thin strips in half; make two small cuts at one end of each strip to form the toes. Fold another strip in half; fold in half again. Twist slightly to form the tail.

4: Attach the Paws and Tail

Press the feet onto the body to adhere. Press the tail onto the top rear of the body.

5: Attach the Ears and Collar

Press down lightly on each end of the remaining dough strip to form the ears; attach to the head. Place 1 thin slice of roasted red bell pepper behind the ears to make the collar.

6: Decorate with Poppy Seed

Lightly wet your finger with water; press into bowl of poppy seed. Press seed on the dog to form spots. Bake 10 to 12 minutes or until golden brown; cool 5 minutes.

gorgonzola, fig and walnut tartlets

prep time: **20 Minutes** • start to finish: **35 Minutes** • **24 tartlets**

1 Pillsbury refrigerated pie crust, softened as directed on box

6 dried figs or pitted dates, coarsely chopped (⅓ cup)

1 tablespoon packed dark brown sugar

⅛ to ¼ teaspoon ground cinnamon

¼ cup chopped walnuts

½ cup crumbled Gorgonzola cheese (2 oz)

1 tablespoon honey

1 Heat oven to 425°F. Unroll pie crust on work surface. Using 2-inch cookie cutter, cut 24 rounds from pie crust, rerolling crust scraps if necessary. Gently press 1 round in bottom and up side of each of 24 ungreased mini muffin cups.

2 In small bowl, mix figs, brown sugar, cinnamon and walnuts. Spoon slightly less than 1 teaspoon fig mixture into each cup. Break up any larger pieces of cheese. Top each tartlet with slightly less than 1 teaspoon cheese.

3 Bake 7 to 11 minutes or until bubbly and golden brown. Remove tartlets from pan to serving plate. Drizzle with honey. Serve warm.

1 Tartlet: Calories 60; Total Fat 3.5g (Saturated Fat 1g, Trans Fat 0g); Cholesterol 0mg; Sodium 60mg; Total Carbohydrate 6g (Dietary Fiber 0g); Protein 0g **Exchanges:** ½ Other Carbohydrate, ½ Fat **Carbohydrate Choices:** ½

twisted pretzel bites

prep time: 40 Minutes • **start to finish:** 1 Hour • 60 servings (1 bite and 1 teaspoon dip each)

1 can Pillsbury™ refrigerated classic pizza crust

⅓ cup baking soda

1 egg, slightly beaten

2 teaspoons kosher (coarse) salt

1 jar (10 oz) queso dip, heated

1 Heat oven to 450°F. Spray cookie sheet with cooking spray. Unroll dough on lightly floured work surface. Cut into 60 (3x½-inch) strips. With hands, roll each strip into rope about 5 inches long. Tie each strip into a knot. Place on cookie sheet.

2 In 4-quart saucepan, heat 5 cups water and the baking soda to boiling. Drop dough knots, 6 at a time, into boiling water. Cook about 30 seconds or until dough looks slightly puffy and dimpled. Using slotted spoon, remove knots from water. Return to cookie sheet and place about ½ inch apart. Brush dough with egg. Sprinkle with salt.

3 Bake 10 to 12 minutes or until well browned. Immediately remove to cooling rack. Cool 5 minutes. Serve warm with queso dip.

1 Serving: Calories 24; Total Fat 1g (Saturated Fat 0g, Trans Fat 0g); Cholesterol 0mg; Sodium 218mg; Total Carbohydrate 4g (Dietary Fiber 0g); Protein 1g **Exchanges:** ½ Starch **Carbohydrate Choices:** ½

spicy churro crescent bites

prep time: 20 Minutes • start to finish: 25 Minutes • 8 servings

1 can (8 oz) Pillsbury Crescent Recipe Creations refrigerated seamless dough sheet

¼ cup orange marmalade

¼ teaspoon ground red pepper (cayenne)

1 tablespoon honey butter spread, softened (from 6.5-oz container)

1½ teaspoons cinnamon sugar

⅔ cup chocolate-flavored hazelnut spread

½ cup whipping cream

1 Heat oven to 375°F. Spray large cookie sheet with cooking spray. Unroll dough sheet on cookie sheet; press into 14x8-inch rectangle.

2 In small bowl, stir marmalade and ⅛ teaspoon of the red pepper until well blended. Spoon marmalade mixture lengthwise over half of dough to within ¾ inch of edges. Carefully lift and fold plain half of dough rectangle over marmalade; pinch edges to seal. Brush top of dough with honey butter spread.

3 Bake 10 to 14 minutes or until puffed and golden brown. Cool on cookie sheet 2 minutes; remove to cooling rack. In small bowl, mix remaining ⅛ teaspoon red pepper and the cinnamon sugar; sprinkle evenly over top.

4 Meanwhile, in 1-quart saucepan, mix hazelnut spread and cream. Cook over medium heat 4 to 5 minutes, stirring frequently, until mixture is warm. DO NOT BOIL.

5 Carefully transfer baked dough to cutting board. With serrated knife, cut in half lengthwise. Make 12 crosswise cuts to make 24 strips. Serve warm with chocolate mixture for dipping.

1 Serving: Calories 340; Total Fat 20g (Saturated Fat 8g, Trans Fat 0g); Cholesterol 25mg; Sodium 260mg; Total Carbohydrate 35g (Dietary Fiber 0g); Protein 3g **Exchanges:** 1 Starch, 1½ Other Carbohydrate, 4 Fat **Carbohydrate Choices:** 2

grands! cheesy olive poppers

prep time: 25 Minutes • **start to finish:** 45 Minutes • 20 appetizers

1 package (3 oz) cream cheese, softened

½ teaspoon Sriracha or hot pepper sauce

1 can (10.2 oz) Pillsbury Grands! Flaky Layers refrigerated buttermilk or original biscuits (5 biscuits)

20 small pimiento-stuffed green olives, drained

1 egg, beaten

Poppy seed, if desired

1 Heat oven to 350°F. Spray cookie sheet with cooking spray.

2 In small bowl, mix cream cheese and Sriracha sauce.

3 Separate dough into 5 biscuits. Cut each biscuit into quarters. Flatten each dough piece enough to hold filling. Spoon about ¾ teaspoon cream cheese mixture in center of each; top with 1 olive. Wrap dough around olive; pinch seams tightly to seal. Place on cookie sheet. Brush each with egg; sprinkle with poppy seed.

4 Bake 10 to 15 minutes or until golden brown. Let stand 5 minutes. Serve warm.

1 Appetizer: Calories 70; Total Fat 4g (Saturated Fat 1.5g, Trans Fat 0.5g); Cholesterol 15mg; Sodium 210mg; Total Carbohydrate 7g (Dietary Fiber 0g); Protein 1g **Exchanges:** ½ Starch, ½ Fat **Carbohydrate Choices:** ½

Easy Success Tip

Be sure the olives are drained well to make the dough easier to seal.

cheesy sriracha corn dog poppers

prep time: **20 Minutes** • start to finish: **35 Minutes** • **24 appetizers**

1 can (8 oz) Pillsbury Crescent Recipe Creations refrigerated seamless dough sheet or 1 can (8 oz) Pillsbury refrigerated crescent dinner rolls (8 rolls)

2 hot dogs, each cut into 12 slices

4 teaspoons Sriracha sauce

2 (1 oz each) Cheddar cheese sticks, each cut into 12 pieces

2 tablespoons cornmeal

Ketchup or salsa, if desired

1 Heat oven to 350°F. Unroll dough (if using crescent roll dough, press perforations to seal). Cut into 24 squares, 6 rows by 4 rows.

2 For each popper, place hot dog slice in center of dough square. Top with a drop of Sriracha sauce and 1 cheese piece. Pull corners up and pinch to seal. Holding seam side down, brush top and sides with Sriracha sauce. Roll in cornmeal, and place seam side down on ungreased cookie sheet. Repeat to make 24 poppers.

3 Bake 12 to 15 minutes or until golden brown. Serve warm with ketchup or salsa.

1 Appetizer: Calories 60; Total Fat 3.5g (Saturated Fat 1.5g, Trans Fat 0g); Cholesterol 0mg; Sodium 150mg; Total Carbohydrate 5g (Dietary Fiber 0g); Protein 1g **Exchanges:** ½ Starch, ½ Fat **Carbohydrate Choices:** ½

Easy Success Tips

For added heat, add some Sriracha sauce to ketchup for dipping.

Too spicy? Reduce the amount of Sriracha sauce.

beer cheese-stuffed pretzels

prep time: **15 Minutes** • start to finish: **30 Minutes** • **4 pretzels**

1 can Pillsbury refrigerated classic pizza crust

½ cup shredded Cheddar cheese (2 oz)

1 egg

1 bottle (12 oz) stout beer

¼ cup baking soda

1 teaspoon coarse (kosher or sea) salt

1 Heat oven to 400°F. Spray large cookie sheet with cooking spray, or line with cooking parchment paper.

2 Unroll dough onto lightly floured work surface. Roll dough into 14x12-inch rectangle. Using pizza cutter, cut dough lengthwise into 4 strips.

3 Along long edge of each dough strip, spread 2 tablespoons of the cheese. Stretch dough over filling; brush edges with water, and pinch to seal. Pick up ends and gently stretch each dough rope to 24 inches long.

4 To make pretzel shape, form each rope into U shape. Twist ends twice. Press down dough where dough overlaps in an X. Pick ends up and fold over so they rest over bottom of U shape. Tuck one end under dough at bottom of U shape; other end lies over dough at bottom of U shape.

5 In small bowl, beat egg and 1 tablespoon of the beer with whisk until blended; set aside.

6 In large microwavable bowl, microwave remaining beer uncovered on High 1 minute 30 seconds or until hot. Slowly add baking soda; stir until dissolved. Dip each pretzel, 1 at a time, into beer and soda mixture. Remove with large pancake turner or slotted spoon; place on cooling rack. Let stand at room temperature 5 minutes.

7 Brush pretzels with egg mixture, and sprinkle with salt. Carefully transfer to cookie sheet. Bake 11 to 15 minutes or until tops of pretzels are dark golden brown.

1 Pretzel: Calories 330; Total Fat 9g (Saturated Fat 4g, Trans Fat 0g); Cholesterol 60mg; Sodium 2340mg; Total Carbohydrate 48g (Dietary Fiber 1g); Protein 12g **Exchanges:** 3 Starch, ½ High-Fat Meat, ½ Fat **Carbohydrate Choices:** 3

mexican snack squares

prep time: 20 Minutes • start to finish: 2 Hours • 48 appetizers

2 cans (8 oz each) Pillsbury refrigerated crescent dinner rolls (8 rolls each) or 2 cans (8 oz each) Pillsbury Crescent Recipe Creations refrigerated seamless dough sheet

1 can (16 oz) refried beans

1 cup sour cream

2 tablespoons taco seasoning mix (from 1-oz package)

1½ cups shredded Cheddar cheese (6 oz)

½ cup sliced green onions (8 medium)

½ cup chopped green bell pepper

1 cup chopped seeded tomato

½ cup sliced ripe olives

Chunky-style salsa, if desired

1 Heat oven to 375°F. If using crescent rolls, unroll both cans of dough. Separate into 4 long rectangles. Place crosswise in ungreased 15x10x1-inch pan; press in bottom and 1 inch up sides to form crust. Firmly press perforations to seal. If using dough sheets, unroll both cans of dough. Place crosswise in ungreased 15x10x1-inch pan; press in bottom and 1 inch up sides to form crust.

2 Bake 14 to 19 minutes or until golden brown. Cool.

3 Spread refried beans over cooled baked crust to within ½ inch of edges. In small bowl, mix sour cream and taco seasoning mix. Spread sour cream mixture over beans. Sprinkle evenly with cheese, green onions, bell pepper, tomato and olives. Cover; refrigerate 1 hour. Cut into 8 rows by 6 rows. Serve with salsa.

1 Appetizer: Calories 70; Total Fat 4.5g (Saturated Fat 2g, Trans Fat 0.5g); Cholesterol 10mg; Sodium 180mg; Total Carbohydrate 6g (Dietary Fiber 0g); Protein 2g **Exchanges:** ½ Other Carbohydrate, 1 Fat **Carbohydrate Choices:** ½

mexican confetti pinwheels

prep time: 15 Minutes • **start to finish:** 35 Minutes • 24 pinwheels

1 can (8 oz) Pillsbury refrigerated crescent dinner rolls (8 rolls)

¼ cup nacho cheese dip

⅓ cup finely chopped red bell pepper (¼ medium)

⅓ cup chopped green onions (about 5 medium)

1 Heat oven to 350°F. Unroll dough and separate into 4 rectangles; firmly press perforations to seal.

2 Spread cheese dip over each rectangle to within ¼ inch of edges. Sprinkle with bell pepper and green onions.

3 Starting with one short side, roll up each rectangle; press edge to seal. With serrated knife, cut each roll into 6 slices; place cut side down on ungreased cookie sheet.

4 Bake 13 to 17 minutes or until edges are golden brown. Immediately remove from cookie sheet. Serve warm.

1 Pinwheel: Calories 40; Total Fat 2g (Saturated Fat 1g, Trans Fat 0g); Cholesterol 0mg; Sodium 150mg; Total Carbohydrate 5g (Dietary Fiber 0g); Protein 1g **Exchanges:** ½ Fat **Carbohydrate Choices:** 0

Easy Success Tip

Try chopped green or yellow bell pepper mixed with the red bell pepper for lively colorful pinwheels.

coconut shrimp appetizer squares

prep time: 15 Minutes • **start to finish:** 35 Minutes • 16 appetizers

1 can Pillsbury refrigerated classic pizza crust

½ cup apricot preserves

1 tablespoon Dijon mustard

1 to 2 teaspoons hot pepper sauce

½ lb uncooked deveined peeled large shrimp, thawed if frozen, tail shells removed, coarsely chopped

1½ cups corn flakes cereal, crushed to ¾ cup

½ cup sweetened coconut

1 Heat oven to 400°F. Spray dark or nonstick cookie sheet with cooking spray. Unroll dough on cookie sheet; press into 12x9-inch rectangle.

2 In small bowl, mix preserves, mustard and pepper sauce until well blended. Spread evenly over dough to within ¼ inch of edges. Top with shrimp. In another small bowl, mix cereal crumbs and coconut; sprinkle over shrimp.

3 Bake 12 to 18 minutes or until golden brown. Serve warm.

1 Appetizer: Calories 120; Total Fat 2g (Saturated Fat 1g, Trans Fat 0g); Cholesterol 20mg; Sodium 330mg; Total Carbohydrate 22g (Dietary Fiber 0g); Protein 4g
Exchanges: 1½ Other Carbohydrate, ½ Very Lean Meat, ½ Fat **Carbohydrate Choices:** 1½

Cilantro Tuna Melts (page 104)

CHAPTER 2

sandwiches

grands! mu shu chicken hand pies

prep time: 20 Minutes • **start to finish:** 55 Minutes • 8 hand pies

1 cup diced cooked chicken breast

2 oz uncooked rice stick noodles, cooked as directed on package, drained

½ cup plum sauce

½ cup sliced green onions (8 medium)

1 can (16.3 oz) Pillsbury Grands! refrigerated biscuits (8 biscuits)

1 Heat oven to 375°F. Lightly grease cookie sheet with shortening or cooking spray.

2 In 2-quart saucepan, heat chicken, cooked rice noodles, plum sauce and ¼ cup of the green onions over medium heat, stirring occasionally, until hot.

3 Separate dough into 8 biscuits. Press or roll each to form 6-inch round. Place on cookie sheet. Using fork to help separate noodles, place about ¼ cup meat mixture in center of each round. Fold dough in half over filling; press edges with fork to seal.

4 Bake 20 to 24 minutes or until golden brown. Cool 10 minutes. Top with remaining green onions. Serve warm.

1 Hand Pie: Calories 270; Total Fat 9g (Saturated Fat 2.5g, Trans Fat 2g); Cholesterol 15mg; Sodium 660mg; Total Carbohydrate 40g (Dietary Fiber 0g); Protein 8g **Exchanges:** 1½ Starch, 1 Other Carbohydrate, ½ Very Lean Meat, 1½ Fat **Carbohydrate Choices:** 2½

Easy Success Tip

Finish off this Asian-inspired meal with some delicious stir-fried vegetables. Any extra plum sauce can be added to the veggies for extra flavor!

easy weeknight chicken pot pie turnovers

prep time: 15 Minutes • **start to finish:** 35 Minutes • 4 turnovers

1 can (18 oz) creamy roasted garlic with chicken stock cooking sauce

1½ cups frozen mixed vegetables

1½ cups chopped deli rotisserie chicken

½ cup plain mashed potato mix (dry)

½ teaspoon salt

⅛ teaspoon pepper

1 box Pillsbury refrigerated pie crusts, softened as directed on box

1 egg, beaten, if desired

1 Heat oven to 425°F. In 2-quart saucepan, heat cooking sauce and frozen vegetables over medium heat until warm. Stir in chicken, dry potatoes, salt and pepper; stir until thickened.

2 Remove pie crusts from pouches; unroll on work surface. Cut each crust in half; place halves on ungreased cookie sheet. Top 1 side of each crust half with 1 cup of the chicken mixture. Fold dough over filling; press edges with fork to seal. Cut several slits in top of each turnover to allow steam to escape. Brush with egg.

3 Bake 15 to 25 minutes or until golden brown. Let stand 5 minutes before serving.

1 Turnover: Calories 650; Total Fat 34g (Saturated Fat 13g, Trans Fat 0g); Cholesterol 110mg; Sodium 1550mg; Total Carbohydrate 61g (Dietary Fiber 2g); Protein 24g **Exchanges:** 1½ Starch, 2½ Other Carbohydrate, ½ Vegetable, 1½ Very Lean Meat, 1 Lean Meat, 6 Fat

cashew chicken twists with spicy orange sauce

prep time: 15 Minutes • **start to finish:** 30 Minutes • 6 servings (2 twists each)

12 uncooked chicken breast tenders (not breaded) (about 1¼ lb)

¼ cup sweet ginger garlic seasoning

1 can Pillsbury refrigerated original breadsticks

¼ cup finely chopped roasted salted cashews

⅔ cup orange marmalade

1½ teaspoons Sriracha sauce

2 teaspoons soy sauce

1 Heat oven to 375°F. Spray large cookie sheet with cooking spray. In large resealable food-storage plastic bag, place chicken tenders and seasoning; shake bag to coat. Set aside.

2 Unroll dough. Sprinkle 2 tablespoons of the cashews over dough; press in lightly. Turn dough over; sprinkle with remaining cashews. Separate dough into 12 breadsticks.

3 Wrap 1 breadstick around each chicken tender (dough will not completely cover chicken). Place 1 inch apart on cookie sheet.

4 Bake 15 to 20 minutes or until golden brown and thermometer inserted in center of chicken reads 165°F.

5 Meanwhile, in small bowl, mix marmalade, Sriracha sauce and soy sauce until well blended. Serve with chicken twists.

1 Serving: Calories 400; Total Fat 8g (Saturated Fat 1.5g, Trans Fat 0g); Cholesterol 60mg; Sodium 1050mg; Total Carbohydrate 55g (Dietary Fiber 0g); Protein 27g **Exchanges:** 2 Starch, 1½ Other Carbohydrate, 3 Very Lean Meat, 1 Fat **Carbohydrate Choices:** 3½

Easy Success Tip

If you can't find the sweet ginger garlic seasoning, use a mixture of 2 tablespoons toasted sesame seed, 1 tablespoon sugar, 1 tablespoon ground ginger, 1 teaspoon garlic salt and 1 teaspoon dried parsley flakes.

chicken tikka masala pies

prep time: **20 Minutes** • start to finish: **50 Minutes** • **4 pies**

1 cup diced cooked chicken breast

½ cup diced green bell pepper

½ cup tikka masala sauce

1 can Pillsbury refrigerated classic pizza crust

¼ cup chopped fresh cilantro leaves

1 Heat oven to 375°F. Lightly spray cookie sheet with cooking spray.

2 In 2-quart saucepan, mix chicken, bell pepper and sauce. Cook over medium heat, stirring occasionally, until bell pepper is soft.

3 Unroll dough on cookie sheet. Starting at center, press out dough to 14x11-inch rectangle; cut into 4 (7x5½-inch) rectangles. Spoon about ⅓ cup filling onto half of each rectangle, spreading to within ½ inch of edge. Fold dough in half over filling; press edges firmly with fork to seal.

4 Bake 22 to 25 minutes or until golden brown. Cool 10 minutes. Sprinkle with cilantro.

1 Pie: Calories 320; Total Fat 10g (Saturated Fat 2.5g, Trans Fat 0g); Cholesterol 30mg; Sodium 630mg; Total Carbohydrate 40g (Dietary Fiber 2g); Protein 17g **Exchanges:** 2 Starch, ½ Other Carbohydrate, 1½ Very Lean Meat, 1½ Fat **Carbohydrate Choices:** 2½

Easy Success Tip

Tikka masala is a popular Indian dish, commonly made with chicken. Look for jars of tikka masala sauce in the ethnic foods aisle of the supermarket.

chicken and spinach biscuit gyros

prep time: 30 Minutes • **start to finish:** 30 Minutes • 8 sandwiches

1 **box (9 oz) frozen chopped spinach**

1 **lb ground chicken**

2 **teaspoons finely chopped garlic**

1 **teaspoon salt**

1 **can (16.3 oz) Pillsbury Grands! Homestyle refrigerated buttermilk biscuits (8 biscuits)**

1 **small red onion, thinly sliced**

1 **large tomato, sliced, each slice cut in half**

1 **container (12 oz) tzatziki**

1 Microwave frozen spinach as directed on box, 3 to 4 minutes to thaw. Squeeze dry with paper towels. In medium bowl, mix spinach, chicken, garlic and salt. Shape into 8 (6x1-inch) logs. Heat 12-inch nonstick skillet over medium-low heat. Cook logs in skillet 5 minutes; turn. Cover and reduce heat to low; cook 10 minutes. Uncover; cook about 5 minutes longer or until thermometer inserted in center of logs reads 165°F and meat is browned.

2 Meanwhile, spray 11-inch griddle or 12-inch skillet with cooking spray; heat over medium-low heat until hot. Separate dough into 8 biscuits. Place 2 biscuits on waxed paper; flatten slightly. Cover with waxed paper; roll each biscuit into 8x4½-inch oval. Place on griddle. Cook 2 to 4 minutes on each side or until golden brown and no longer doughy. Repeat with remaining biscuits. Cover with foil and keep warm.

3 Place chicken log in center of each biscuit flatbread. Top with onion slices, tomato slices and tzatziki. Fold flatbread around filling.

1 Sandwich: Calories 280; Total Fat 12g (Saturated Fat 4.5g, Trans Fat 0g); Cholesterol 35mg; Sodium 690mg; Total Carbohydrate 30g (Dietary Fiber 2g); Protein 12g **Exchanges:** 1½ Starch, ½ Other Carbohydrate, ½ Vegetable, 1 Lean Meat, 1½ Fat **Carbohydrate Choices:** 2

Easy Success Tips

Tzatziki is a yogurt sauce mixed with cucumbers. If you can't find tzatziki, look for Greek yogurt veggie dip containing cucumber, dill and feta at your grocery store.

Moisten your hands with water to easily shape the chicken mixture into logs.

chicken and ham slab sandwiches

prep time: 10 Minutes • **start to finish:** 35 Minutes • 4 servings

1 can Pillsbury refrigerated classic pizza crust

1 can (18 oz) creamy Parmesan basil cooking sauce

2 cups shredded deli rotisserie chicken

½ cup diced cooked ham

4 slices (1½ oz each) provolone cheese

Garnishes, If Desired

Chopped seeded tomato

Chopped fresh or dried basil leaves

1 Heat oven to 400°F. Spray large cookie sheet with cooking spray. Unroll dough on cookie sheet; press into 12x10-inch rectangle.

2 Reserve 3 tablespoons cooking sauce from can; set aside. In medium bowl, stir ¾ cup of the sauce, the chicken and ham until well blended. Spread chicken mixture on half of dough to within 1 inch of edges. Arrange cheese slices, slightly overlapping, over chicken mixture. Fold dough over chicken mixture and cheese; press edges with fingers to seal and then press edges again with tines of fork. Brush reserved 3 tablespoons sauce over dough. Cut 4 evenly spaced ½-inch slits in dough.

3 Bake 15 to 17 minutes or until golden brown. Let stand 5 minutes. Meanwhile, heat remaining sauce until hot. Cut sandwich into 4 pieces. Top each piece with tomato and basil. Serve with sauce for dipping.

1 Serving: Calories 630; Total Fat 28g (Saturated Fat 12g, Trans Fat 0.5g); Cholesterol 105mg; Sodium 2090mg; Total Carbohydrate 52g (Dietary Fiber 2g); Protein 44g **Exchanges:** 3 Starch, ½ Other Carbohydrate, 2½ Very Lean Meat, 1 Lean Meat, 1½ High-Fat Meat, 2 Fat **Carbohydrate Choices:** 3½

chicken-bacon-portabella burgers

prep time: 30 Minutes • **start to finish:** 50 Minutes • 5 sandwiches

1 can (10.2 oz) Pillsbury Grands! Homestyle refrigerated buttermilk biscuits (5 biscuits)

1 box (9 oz) frozen chopped spinach

10 slices uncooked bacon

¼ cup chopped green onions (4 medium)

5 medium whole portabella mushrooms (about 5-inch diameter), stems removed and chopped

2 cups shredded deli rotisserie chicken

¼ teaspoon salt

¼ teaspoon pepper

5 slices (1 oz each) Monterey Jack cheese

Additional chopped green onions, if desired

1 Heat oven to 350°F. Separate dough into 5 biscuits; press each into 4-inch round. Place 2 inches apart on ungreased large cookie sheet. Bake 12 to 15 minutes or until golden brown.

2 Meanwhile, microwave spinach as directed on box. Drain well; set aside.

3 In 12-inch nonstick skillet, cook bacon until crisp; drain on paper towels. Reserve 2 tablespoons bacon drippings. Reserve 5 bacon slices; set aside.

4 Chop remaining 5 bacon slices. In same skillet, add the reserved bacon drippings, the chopped bacon, green onions and mushroom stems. Cook over medium heat 2 to 3 minutes, stirring occasionally, until onions are crisp-tender. Stir in spinach, chicken, salt and pepper. Cook 2 to 3 minutes or until thoroughly heated.

5 Line large cookie sheet with cooking parchment paper. Place mushrooms on cookie sheet, top side down. Spoon chicken mixture on mushroom caps. Bake 14 to 18 minutes or until mushrooms are tender. Remove from oven; top each with cheese slice. Bake 2 to 5 minutes longer or until cheese is melted.

6 Split each biscuit horizontally. Place 1 mushroom on bottom half of each biscuit. Top with reserved bacon slice and top half of biscuit. Garnish with additional chopped green onions.

1 Sandwich: Calories 500; Total Fat 27g (Saturated Fat 10g, Trans Fat 4g); Cholesterol 90mg; Sodium 1530mg; Total Carbohydrate 31g (Dietary Fiber 2g); Protein 34g **Exchanges:** 1 Starch, 3 Vegetable, 2½ Very Lean Meat, 1 High-Fat Meat, 3½ Fat **Carbohydrate Choices:** 2

thai turkey burgers with peanut sauce

prep time: 30 Minutes • **start to finish:** 40 Minutes • 6 servings

1 can (16.3 oz) Pillsbury Grands! Flaky Layers refrigerated original biscuits (8 biscuits)

½ cup natural creamy peanut butter spread

3 tablespoons soy sauce

4 tablespoons sweet chili sauce

Grated peel (1½ teaspoons) and juice (2½ tablespoons) of 1 small lime

¼ cup water

20 oz ground turkey

¼ teaspoon pepper

1 box (9 oz) frozen chopped spinach

¼ teaspoon salt

1 Heat oven to 350°F. Bake biscuits as directed on can. Cool.

2 Meanwhile, in small bowl, mix peanut butter spread, 1 tablespoon of the soy sauce, 2 tablespoons of the chili sauce, the lime peel, lime juice and water. Set aside.

3 In food processor, place 2 biscuits. Cover; process 15 to 20 seconds with on-and-off pulses or until consistency of bread crumbs. In large bowl, mix bread crumbs, turkey, ⅛ teaspoon of the pepper, remaining 2 tablespoons soy sauce, and remaining 2 tablespoons chili sauce. Shape mixture into 6 patties, 4 inches in diameter.

4 In 12-inch nonstick skillet, cook patties over medium heat 6 to 10 minutes, turning 2 to 3 times, until meat thermometer inserted in center of patties reads 165°F.

5 Meanwhile, microwave frozen spinach as directed on box. Cool slightly; squeeze to drain. In small bowl, mix spinach, salt and remaining ⅛ teaspoon pepper.

6 Split the 6 remaining biscuits. Spread 1 tablespoon peanut sauce on bottom of each biscuit. Top with burger, spinach and biscuit tops. Serve with remaining sauce.

1 Serving: Calories 590; Total Fat 34g (Saturated Fat 8g, Trans Fat 3g); Cholesterol 75mg; Sodium 1560mg; Total Carbohydrate 43g (Dietary Fiber 3g); Protein 28g **Exchanges:** 1 Starch, 1½ Other Carbohydrate, ½ Vegetable, 2½ Medium-Fat Meat, 1 High-Fat Meat, 2½ Fat **Carbohydrate Choices:** 3

spicy sweet turkey rolls

prep time: 25 Minutes • **start to finish:** 45 Minutes • **5 servings**

½ cup coarsely chopped orange bell pepper

1 can (8 oz) pineapple chunks in juice, drained, juice reserved

5 tablespoons red wine vinegar

¾ cup plus 2 tablespoons orange marmalade medley

⅛ teaspoon salt

¼ teaspoon ground red pepper (cayenne)

10 oz ground turkey

¼ teaspoon salt

¼ teaspoon black pepper

1 can (10.2 oz) Pillsbury Grands! Homestyle refrigerated buttermilk biscuits (5 biscuits)

1 Heat oven to 350°F. Line large cookie sheet with cooking parchment paper. In food processor, place bell pepper and pineapple chunks. Cover; process with on-and-off pulses until finely chopped. Stop machine and scrape sides of bowl, if necessary.

2 In 1-quart saucepan, mix reserved pineapple juice, 4 tablespoons of the vinegar, ¾ cup of the marmalade, ⅛ teaspoon salt and ⅛ teaspoon of the red pepper. Heat to boiling over medium-high heat. Reduce heat to low; simmer about 15 minutes or until sauce thickens and is reduced to 1 cup.

3 Meanwhile, in 10-inch skillet, mix pineapple mixture, turkey, ¼ teaspoon salt, the black pepper and remaining ⅛ teaspoon red pepper. Cook over medium heat 5 minutes, stirring occasionally, until turkey is no longer pink. Add remaining 1 tablespoon red wine vinegar and remaining 2 tablespoons marmalade. Cook 2 to 4 minutes longer or until most of the liquid has evaporated. Cool 5 minutes.

4 Separate dough into 5 biscuits; pat each biscuit into 7½x4½-inch oval. Spoon turkey mixture down center of each biscuit. Bring long sides of biscuit over filling, overlapping slightly in center. Fold up short sides to enclose filling; pinch edges to seal. Place seam side down 2 inches apart on cookie sheet. Prick each top 3 times with toothpick.

5 Bake 15 to 20 minutes or until golden brown. Serve with sauce.

1 Serving: Calories 460; Total Fat 14g (Saturated Fat 3.5g, Trans Fat 3.5g); Cholesterol 45mg; Sodium 790mg; Total Carbohydrate 70g (Dietary Fiber 0g); Protein 13g **Exchanges:** 2 Starch, 2½ Other Carbohydrate, 1 Medium-Fat Meat, 1½ Fat **Carbohydrate Choices:** 4½

turkey and pear sandwiches with spicy orange marmalade

prep time: 25 Minutes • **start to finish:** 30 Minutes • 4 servings

1 can Pillsbury refrigerated crusty French loaf

⅔ cup orange marmalade

5 tablespoons spicy brown mustard

4 turkey cutlets (about 4 oz each)

¼ teaspoon salt

⅛ teaspoon pepper

2 small firm ripe pears, cored, thinly sliced

4 oz smoked Gouda cheese, sliced

4 cup loosely packed mixed greens

1 Heat oven to 350°F. Spray large cookie sheet with cooking spray. Cut loaf of dough crosswise into 4 pieces. Place pieces seam side down on cookie sheet. Using sharp or serrated knife, cut 2 diagonal ¼-inch-deep slashes in top of each piece. Bake 18 to 20 minutes or until golden brown. Remove from cookie sheet to cooling rack; cool 10 minutes.

2 Meanwhile, in small bowl, mix marmalade and 2 tablespoons of the mustard. Set aside.

3 Spray 12-inch skillet with cooking spray. Lightly sprinkle cutlets with salt and pepper. Brush both sides of cutlets with remaining 3 tablespoons mustard. Cook cutlets over medium heat 2 to 3 minutes or until browned. Turn; top each cutlet with pears. Cook 2 to 3 minutes longer or until turkey is no longer pink in center and pears are tender. Top pears with cheese. Cover; remove from heat and let stand 2 to 3 minutes or until cheese is melted.

4 Cut each roll in half horizontally. Spread 2 tablespoons of the marmalade mixture over cut sides of rolls. On bottoms of rolls, place greens, cutlets and tops of rolls. Serve with remaining sauce.

1 Serving: Calories 620; Total Fat 12g (Saturated Fat 6g, Trans Fat 0g); Cholesterol 110mg; Sodium 1120mg; Total Carbohydrate 86g (Dietary Fiber 4g); Protein 41g **Exchanges:** 2½ Starch, ½ Fruit, 2½ Other Carbohydrate, 1 Vegetable, 3½ Very Lean Meat, 1 High-Fat Meat **Carbohydrate Choices:** 6

turkey and cauliflower open-face sandwiches

prep time: 20 Minutes • **start to finish:** 55 Minutes • 4 sandwiches

1 can Pillsbury refrigerated crusty French loaf

2 boxes (10 oz each) frozen cauliflower and cheese sauce

2 teaspoons harissa sauce

2 cloves garlic, finely chopped

¾ lb thinly sliced deli turkey breast

4 lemon wedges

6 fresh basil leaves, thinly sliced

Pepper, if desired

1 Heat oven to 350°F. Spray large cookie sheet with cooking spray.

2 Cut loaf of dough in half crosswise to make 2 loaves. Place loaves seam side down and 3 inches apart on cookie sheet. Using sharp knife, cut 3 diagonal ½-inch-deep slashes in top of each loaf. Bake 23 to 25 minutes or until golden brown. Cool.

3 Meanwhile, microwave both pouches of cauliflower as directed on box, microwaving 8 to 9 minutes. In medium bowl, mix cauliflower, harissa sauce and garlic.

4 Set oven control to broil. With serrated knife, cut loaves in half horizontally; place cut side up on same cookie sheet. Place turkey on each. Top with cauliflower mixture. Broil 4 to 5 inches from heat 4 to 6 minutes or until thoroughly heated.

5 Squeeze lemon wedge over each open-face sandwich. Sprinkle with basil and a dash of pepper.

1 Sandwich: Calories 360; Total Fat 8g (Saturated Fat 3g, Trans Fat 0g); Cholesterol 40mg; Sodium 2080mg; Total Carbohydrate 48g (Dietary Fiber 1g); Protein 24g **Exchanges:** 1½ Starch, 1½ Other Carbohydrate, 1 Vegetable, 2½ Very Lean Meat, 1 Fat **Carbohydrate Choices:** 3

Easy Success Tip

Harissa sauce is a Tunisian hot chili sauce flavored with chiles, garlic, caraway, coriander and cumin. If you can't find it, you can substitute hot chili sauce.

grands! beef and stout hand pies

prep time: 25 Minutes • **start to finish:** 40 Minutes • 8 hand pies

½ lb lean (at least 80%) ground beef

½ cup finely chopped onion (1 medium)

1 cup diced fresh sweet potatoes

½ cup Irish stout

½ teaspoon salt

⅛ teaspoon pepper

1 can (16.3 oz) Pillsbury Grands! Flaky Layers refrigerated original biscuits (8 biscuits)

1 Heat oven to 375°F. Grease cookie sheet with shortening or cooking spray.

2 In 10-inch skillet, cook beef and onion over medium heat 8 to 10 minutes, stirring occasionally, until beef is thoroughly cooked; drain. Stir in sweet potatoes, stout, salt and pepper. Heat to boiling. Reduce heat to low; cover and simmer about 8 minutes or until vegetables are tender. Uncover; cook 1 to 2 minutes longer or until liquid is evaporated.

3 Separate dough into 8 biscuits. Press or roll each to form 6-inch round. Place on cookie sheet. Spoon about ¼ cup meat mixture in center of each round. Fold dough in half over filling; press with fork to seal.

4 Bake 12 to 15 minutes or until golden brown.

1 Hand Pie: Calories 250; Total Fat 11g (Saturated Fat 3g, Trans Fat 2g); Cholesterol 20mg; Sodium 710mg; Total Carbohydrate 29g (Dietary Fiber 0g); Protein 8g **Exchanges:** 1½ Starch, ½ Other Carbohydrate, ½ Medium-Fat Meat, 1½ Fat **Carbohydrate Choices:** 2

Easy Success Tip

A fresh green salad with the hand pies and chocolate ice cream for dessert are all you need to turn these hearty snacks into a meal.

livia's peruvian empanadas

prep time: 30 Minutes • **start to finish:** 1 Hour • 8 empanadas

1 tablespoon vegetable oil

½ lb beef sirloin steak, cut into ¼-inch cubes

1 small onion, cut in half, sliced

1 plum (Roma) tomato, seeded, chopped

1 teaspoon soy sauce

1 teaspoon red wine vinegar

¼ teaspoon pepper

1 box Pillsbury refrigerated pie crusts, softened as directed on box

1 Heat oven to 450°F. In 10-inch skillet, heat oil over medium-high heat. Add beef. Cook, stirring frequently, about 3 minutes or until brown; reserve in medium bowl. In same skillet, cook onion about 3 minutes or until brown. Add tomato, beef, soy sauce, vinegar and pepper. Cook 2 to 3 minutes or until liquid has evaporated. Remove from heat. Cool 5 minutes.

2 On lightly floured work surface, roll each pie crust into 14-inch round. Using 6-inch round plate, cut 3 rounds from each crust. Reroll remaining dough, and cut 2 more 6-inch rounds. Moisten edge of each round with water, and place about 2 tablespoons filling in center. Fold dough in half over filling; press edges with fork to seal. On ungreased cookie sheet, place 2 inches apart. Prick top of each empanada once with fork to vent steam.

3 Bake 10 to 12 minutes or until light golden brown. Cool 10 minutes.

1 Empanada: Calories 250; Total Fat 14g (Saturated Fat 5g, Trans Fat 0g); Cholesterol 15mg; Sodium 300mg; Total Carbohydrate 25g (Dietary Fiber 0g); Protein 5g **Exchanges:** ½ Starch, 1 Other Carbohydrate, ½ Lean Meat, 2½ Fat **Carbohydrate Choices:** 1½

Easy Success Tip

Serve these delicious empanadas with a crispy tossed salad to complete the meal.

big & tasty cheeseburger pockets

prep time: **15 Minutes** • start to finish: **30 Minutes** • **4 pockets**

1 lb lean (at least 80%) ground beef

½ cup ketchup

¼ cup dill pickle relish

1 cup diced American cheese (4 oz)

1 tablespoon yellow mustard

1 can (12 oz) Pillsbury™ Grands!™ Big & Flaky refrigerated crescent dinner rolls (8 rolls)

1 teaspoon sesame seed

1 Heat oven to 375°F. In 10-inch skillet, cook beef over medium heat 8 to 10 minutes, stirring occasionally, until browned and thoroughly cooked; drain. Stir in relish, cheese and mustard. Set aside. Separate dough into 4 rectangles. Place on ungreased cookie sheet. Press each to 8x5 inches, firmly pressing perforations to seal.

2 Divide beef mixture evenly among rectangles. Bring ends up over filling, overlapping about 1 inch. Press edges with fork to seal. Brush each with water, and sprinkle with ¼ teaspoon sesame seed.

3 Bake 13 to 15 minutes or until golden brown. Immediately remove from cookie sheet. Serve warm.

1 Pocket: Calories 640; Total Fat 36g (Saturated Fat 16g, Trans Fat 1g); Cholesterol 95mg; Sodium 1690mg; Total Carbohydrate 47g (Dietary Fiber 1g); Protein 31g **Exchanges:** 1 Starch, 2 Other Carbohydrate, 3 Medium-Fat Meat, 1 High-Fat Meat, 2½ Fat **Carbohydrate Choices:** 3

grands! blt sandwiches

prep time: **20 Minutes** • start to finish: **35 Minutes** • **4 large sandwiches**

1 can (17.3 oz) Pillsbury™ Grands!™ Reduced Fat refrigerated golden wheat biscuits (8 biscuits)

½ cup reduced-fat mayonnaise

4 lettuce leaves

8 large slices tomato

1 lb low-sodium bacon, crisply cooked

1 Heat oven to 350°F. Lightly grease cookie sheets. Separate dough into 8 biscuits. Press or roll each biscuit to form 5½-inch round. Place on cookie sheets.

2 Bake 16 to 18 minutes or until golden brown. Cool slightly.

3 Spread 1 tablespoon mayonnaise on bottom of each biscuit. Top 4 biscuits with 1 lettuce leaf, 2 tomato slices and 4 or 5 slices of bacon each. Top with remaining biscuits, mayonnaise side down.

1 Large Sandwich: Calories 660; Total Fat 39g (Saturated Fat 11g, Trans Fat 0g); Cholesterol 45mg; Sodium 1860mg; Total Carbohydrate 57g (Dietary Fiber 4g); Protein 20g **Exchanges:** 4 Starch, 1 High-Fat Meat, 5½ Fat **Carbohydrate Choices:** 4

Easy Success Tip

These large sandwiches are indeed a meal on their own. But some sliced fresh fruit or even favorite berries are a nice accompaniment.

latvian bacon pierogi

prep time: **25 Minutes** • start to finish: **45 Minutes** • **8 hand pies**

½ lb bacon, chopped

1 cup diced (¼ inch) peeled russet baking potato

1 large onion, chopped (1 cup)

1 can (16.3 oz) Pillsbury Grands! refrigerated biscuits (8 biscuits)

1 Heat oven to 375°F. Lightly grease cookie sheet with shortening or cooking spray.

2 In 10-inch skillet over medium heat, cook bacon until crisp. Remove from skillet with slotted spoon; drain on paper towels. Cook potato and onion in bacon drippings over medium heat until tender; drain on paper towels. In medium bowl, mix potato mixture and cooked bacon.

3 Separate dough into 8 biscuits. Press or roll each to form 6-inch round. Place on cookie sheet. Spoon about ¼ cup bacon mixture in center of each round. Fold dough in half over filling; press with fork to seal.

4 Bake about 15 minutes or until golden brown. Cool 5 minutes. Serve warm.

1 Hand Pie: Calories 250; Total Fat 11g (Saturated Fat 3g, Trans Fat 2g); Cholesterol 10mg; Sodium 720mg; Total Carbohydrate 30g (Dietary Fiber 0g); Protein 6g **Exchanges:** 2 Starch, 2 Fat **Carbohydrate Choices:** 2

Easy Success Tip

Although not as traditional, chopped sweet potatoes can be substituted for the baking potatoes. The result is slightly sweeter but just as delicious!

chorizo-potato puffy tacos

prep time: 30 Minutes • **start to finish:** 35 Minutes • 8 servings (2 tacos each)

1 lb ground pork chorizo

1 bag (11.8 oz) frozen backyard grilled potatoes

1 can (16.3 oz) Pillsbury Grands! Homestyle refrigerated buttermilk biscuits (8 biscuits)

3 medium tomatillos, quartered

2 large avocados, pitted, peeled and cubed

1 cup fresh cilantro, chopped

1 teaspoon salt

1 teaspoon pepper

¾ cup crumbled Cotija (white Mexican) cheese or queso fresco cheese (3 oz)

1 Heat oven to 350°F. In 10-inch skillet, cook chorizo 8 to 10 minutes, stirring occasionally, until thoroughly cooked. Meanwhile, microwave frozen potatoes 5 minutes as directed on bag. Remove from bag, and coarsely chop potatoes. Stir into chorizo. Keep warm.

2 Meanwhile, separate dough into 8 biscuits. Separate each biscuit into 2 layers. Press each layer into 4-inch round. Place on large ungreased cookie sheets. Bake 9 to 11 minutes or until light golden brown, rotating cookie sheets after 5 minutes.

3 Meanwhile, in food processor, place tomatillos, avocados, ½ cup of the cilantro, the salt and pepper. Cover; process 20 to 30 seconds or until smooth.

4 To assemble tacos, gently fold each biscuit in half. Fill each with ¼ cup chorizo mixture and 2 tablespoons tomatillo mixture. Sprinkle with cheese and remaining cilantro.

1 Serving: Calories 450; Total Fat 26g (Saturated Fat 9g, Trans Fat 0g); Cholesterol 45mg; Sodium 1170mg; Total Carbohydrate 37g (Dietary Fiber 3g); Protein 17g **Exchanges:** 1 Starch, 1½ Other Carbohydrate, 1½ Medium-Fat Meat, ½ High-Fat Meat, 3 Fat **Carbohydrate Choices:** 2½

bacon, egg and cheese sandwiches

prep time: 10 Minutes • **start to finish:** 30 Minutes • 8 sandwiches

1 can (8 oz) Pillsbury refrigerated crescent dinner rolls (8 rolls)

8 slices bacon, crisply cooked, crumbled (½ cup)

4 eggs, scrambled

½ cup finely shredded Cheddar cheese (2 oz)

1 egg, beaten, if desired

1 tablespoon cracked black pepper, if desired

1 Heat oven to 350°F. Separate dough into 8 triangles. Top each triangle with bacon, scrambled egg and cheese. Roll up loosely as directed on can. Place on ungreased cookie sheet; curve into crescent shape. Brush with beaten egg and sprinkle with pepper.

2 Bake 18 to 20 minutes or until golden brown.

1 Sandwich: Calories 200; Total Fat 13g (Saturated Fat 5g, Trans Fat 1.5g); Cholesterol 105mg; Sodium 410mg; Total Carbohydrate 12g (Dietary Fiber 0g); Protein 8g **Exchanges:** 1 Starch, ½ Medium-Fat Meat, 2 Fat **Carbohydrate Choices:** 1

Easy Success Tip

It's easy to make scrambled eggs in the microwave. Beat the eggs well in a medium microwavable bowl. Microwave uncovered on High for 1 minute 30 seconds. Stir the cooked outer edges to the center. Microwave 1 to 2 minutes longer or until the eggs are almost set but still moist.

easy sausage grandwiches

prep time: **15 Minutes** • start to finish: **30 Minutes** • **8 sandwiches**

1 can (16.3 oz) Pillsbury Grands! refrigerated biscuits (8 biscuits)

8 small precooked pork sausage patties, thawed

6 eggs, scrambled

8 slices (¾ oz each) American cheese

1 Heat oven to 350°F. Bake biscuits as directed on can.

2 Meanwhile, heat sausage patties as directed on package.

3 Split warm biscuits in half. Top bottom half of each with scrambled egg, sausage and cheese. Cover with top halves of biscuits.

1 Sandwich: Calories 400; Total Fat 25g (Saturated Fat 9g, Trans Fat 3.5g); Cholesterol 185mg; Sodium 1140mg; Total Carbohydrate 26g (Dietary Fiber 0g); Protein 17g **Exchanges:** 1½ Starch, 1½ Lean Meat, 4 Fat **Carbohydrate Choices:** 2

Easy Success Tip

There's no need to go out for breakfast when you can make these warm biscuit sandwiches. Plan to serve them for brunch with a fresh fruit salad and coffee or tea.

breakfast crescent dogs

prep time: 10 Minutes • start to finish: 25 Minutes • 8 servings

1 can (8 oz) Pillsbury refrigerated crescent dinner rolls (8 rolls)

8 fully cooked pork sausage links

¾ cup maple-flavored syrup

1 Heat oven to 375°F. Separate dough into 8 triangles. Wrap 1 dough triangle around each sausage link. Place seam side down on ungreased cookie sheet.

2 Bake 12 to 15 minutes or until golden brown. Serve warm with syrup.

1 Serving: Calories 270; Total Fat 13g (Saturated Fat 4.5g, Trans Fat 1.5g); Cholesterol 15mg; Sodium 380mg; Total Carbohydrate 32g (Dietary Fiber 0g); Protein 5g **Exchanges:** 1½ Starch, ½ Other Carbohydrate, 2½ Fat **Carbohydrate Choices:** 2

Easy Success Tip

Fully cooked breakfast sausage links make this recipe quick and easy for a weekday breakfast. If using uncooked sausage links, just cook them following package directions before wrapping with the dough and baking.

pastrami melt on crusty pretzel rolls

prep time: 30 Minutes • **start to finish:** 45 Minutes • **4 sandwiches**

2 cans Pillsbury refrigerated crusty French loaf

2 tablespoons coarse (kosher or sea) salt

½ cup stone-ground mustard

¼ cup cherry preserves

8 slices (1 oz each) smoked Cheddar cheese

16 slices deli pastrami (about 1 lb)

½ cup bread-and-butter pickle slices, drained

1 Heat oven to 450°F. Spray large cookie sheet with cooking spray. In 4-quart saucepan or Dutch oven, heat 10 cups water to boiling over medium-high heat. Reduce heat to medium-low.

2 Meanwhile, cut each loaf of dough in half crosswise to make 4 pieces. Add 2 pieces at a time to water for 30 seconds. Using tongs or slotted spoon, turn pieces over; simmer 30 seconds longer. Place pieces seam side down on cookie sheet. Repeat with remaining pieces. Sprinkle tops with salt.

3 Bake 15 to 19 minutes or until deep golden brown. Remove to cooling rack. Cool 5 minutes.

4 Meanwhile, in small bowl, beat mustard and preserves with whisk until blended.

5 Cut each roll in half horizontally. Spread cut side of tops with mustard mixture. On bottoms of rolls, place cheese, pastrami, pickles and tops of rolls. Wrap each sandwich in foil.

6 Bake about 10 minutes or until cheese is melted. Cut in half to serve.

1 Sandwich: Calories 860; Total Fat 32g (Saturated Fat 16g, Trans Fat 1g); Cholesterol 130mg; Sodium 6720mg; Total Carbohydrate 93g (Dietary Fiber 1g); Protein 51g **Exchanges:** 5 Starch, 1½ Low-Fat Milk, 3½ Lean Meat, 2 Fat **Carbohydrate Choices:** 6

thai chicken burgers

prep time: 20 Minutes • **start to finish:** 30 Minutes • 8 sandwiches

1 can (16.3 oz) Pillsbury Grands! Homestyle refrigerated buttermilk biscuits (8 biscuits)

1 cup fresh bean sprouts

⅔ cup sliced green onions

1½ lb ground chicken

1 teaspoon salt

½ teaspoon pepper

½ cup water

1 cup crunchy peanut butter

4½ teaspoons hot chili sauce

1½ cups shredded Chinese (napa) cabbage

Chopped green onions, if desired

1 Heat oven to 350°F. Bake biscuits as directed on can; keep warm.

2 Meanwhile, finely chop ½ cup of the bean sprouts; place in large bowl. Add ⅓ cup of the green onions, the chicken, salt and pepper; mix well. Shape mixture into 8 patties, 3½ inches in diameter.

3 In 12-inch nonstick skillet, cook patties over medium-high heat 5 to 7 minutes, turning once, until thermometer inserted in center of patties reads at least 165°F.

4 In 1-quart saucepan, mix water and remaining ½ cup bean sprouts. Heat to boiling; reduce heat to medium-low and simmer about 2 minutes or until sprouts are thoroughly cooked and no longer crisp. Stir in peanut butter and chili sauce; cook, stirring constantly, until thoroughly heated. Remove from heat. Stir in remaining ⅓ cup green onions.

5 Split biscuits in half. Place burgers on bottom of each biscuit. Spoon 2 tablespoons peanut butter mixture over burgers; top with cabbage and biscuit tops. Garnish with green onions. Serve with remaining peanut butter mixture.

1 Sandwich: Calories 500; Total Fat 30g (Saturated Fat 7g, Trans Fat 0g); Cholesterol 50mg; Sodium 1060mg; Total Carbohydrate 36g (Dietary Fiber 3g); Protein 22g **Exchanges:** 2 Other Carbohydrate, ½ Vegetable, 2 Medium-Fat Meat, 1 High-Fat Meat, 2½ Fat **Carbohydrate Choices:** 2½

greek shrimp and feta pies

prep time: 15 Minutes • start to finish: 40 Minutes • 6 hand pies

1 can Pillsbury refrigerated thin pizza crust

¼ lb chopped cooked deveined peeled small shrimp, patted dry with paper towels (¾ cup)

⅓ cup drained chopped artichoke hearts (from 14-oz can), patted dry with paper towels

¼ cup crumbled feta cheese (1 oz)

⅓ cup chopped drained roasted red bell peppers (from a jar), patted dry with paper towels

1 Heat oven to 400°F. Lightly spray cookie sheet with cooking spray.

2 Unroll dough on cookie sheet. Starting at center, press out dough to 15x10-inch rectangle; cut into 6 (5-inch) squares. In medium bowl, mix remaining ingredients. Place about ¼ cup filling in center of each square. Fold dough in half over filling; press edges firmly with fork to seal.

3 Bake about 15 minutes or until golden brown. Cool 10 minutes. Serve warm.

1 Hand Pie: Calories 200; Total Fat 6g (Saturated Fat 2g, Trans Fat 0g); Cholesterol 45mg; Sodium 590mg; Total Carbohydrate 26g (Dietary Fiber 1g); Protein 9g **Exchanges:** 1 Starch, ½ Other Carbohydrate, 1 Very Lean Meat, 1 Fat **Carbohydrate Choices:** 2

Easy Success Tip

If you have trouble finding crumbled feta cheese, you can purchase feta in a block. Simply break off a chunk, and it will be easy to crumble with your fingers.

crescent coulibiac puffs

prep time: **30 Minutes** • start to finish: **1 Hour** • **8 puffs**

8 **oz salmon fillets (about 1 inch thick), skin removed**

2 **cups loosely packed fresh spinach**

4 **oz sliced fresh mushrooms**

1 **can (8 oz) Pillsbury refrigerated crescent dinner rolls (8 rolls)**

3 **tablespoons plain panko crispy bread crumbs**

1 **teaspoon salt**

2 **teaspoons finely grated lemon peel**

1 Heat oven to 375°F. Cut salmon fillet into 8 (1-oz) pieces; dry on paper towels.

2 Heat 10-inch nonstick skillet over medium heat. Add spinach and mushrooms. Cook, stirring occasionally, until spinach wilts and mushrooms are tender. Place in strainer to drain, pressing out as much liquid as possible. Place spinach mixture on cutting board; finely chop. Return chopped mixture to strainer.

3 Separate dough into 8 triangles. For each puff, sprinkle 1 teaspoon of the bread crumbs on dough triangle. Place 1 piece salmon on bread crumbs; sprinkle with ⅛ teaspoon of the salt. Spoon 1 firmly packed tablespoon spinach mixture on top of salmon. Top with ¼ teaspoon of the lemon peel. Wrap dough around salmon, sealing well so mixture is completely covered. Place on ungreased cookie sheet.

4 Bake 17 to 19 minutes or until golden brown. Cool 10 minutes. Serve warm.

1 Puff: Calories 160; Total Fat 8g (Saturated Fat 2.5g, Trans Fat 1.5g); Cholesterol 20mg; Sodium 540mg; Total Carbohydrate 14g (Dietary Fiber 0g); Protein 9g **Exchanges:** ½ Starch, ½ Other Carbohydrate, 1 Lean Meat, 1 Fat **Carbohydrate Choices:** 1

Easy Success Tip

Grated lemon peel adds wonderful flavor without adding extra liquid. After grating, wrap the lemon in plastic wrap, and store in the refrigerator for juicing later.

grands! smoked salmon pastries

prep time: 30 Minutes • start to finish: 50 Minutes • 8 pastries

1 large russet baking potato (about 12 oz)

¾ teaspoon grated lemon peel

1 can (16.3 oz) Pillsbury Grands! Flaky Layers refrigerated original biscuits (8 biscuits)

3 oz very thinly sliced smoked salmon, cut into 8 pieces

¼ cup sliced green onions (4 medium)

1 Heat oven to 375°F. Pierce potato several times with fork to allow steam to escape. Microwave uncovered on High 5 to 6 minutes or until tender. Cool slightly, about 5 minutes. Cut in half lengthwise; scoop out inside into small bowl. Mash with fork. Stir in lemon peel.

2 Separate dough into 8 biscuits. Press or roll each to form 6-inch round. Place on ungreased cookie sheet. Place 1 piece salmon on half of each dough round. Spoon about 2 tablespoons potato mixture over salmon, to within ½ inch of edge. Sprinkle each with 1½ teaspoons green onion. Fold dough in half over filling; press edges with fork to seal.

3 Bake 15 to 18 minutes or until golden brown.

1 Pastry: Calories 220; Total Fat 8g (Saturated Fat 2g, Trans Fat 2g); Cholesterol 0mg; Sodium 630mg; Total Carbohydrate 31g (Dietary Fiber 0g); Protein 5g **Exchanges:** 1½ Starch, ½ Other Carbohydrate, 1½ Fat **Carbohydrate Choices:** 2

Easy Success Tip

Smoked salmon comes in wafer-thin slices. Look for it in the deli section of the supermarket.

Pear and Gorgonzola Pizza (page 146)

CHAPTER 3

pizzas

bbq chicken pizza

prep time: 20 Minutes • start to finish: 40 Minutes • 6 servings (3 pieces each)

1 can Pillsbury refrigerated artisan pizza crust with whole grain

2 cups coarsely chopped cooked chicken breast

¾ cup barbecue sauce

2 cups shredded reduced-fat mozzarella cheese (8 oz)

½ cup thinly sliced red onion

1 tablespoon chopped fresh parsley or cilantro, if desired

1 Heat oven to 400°F for dark or nonstick pan (425°F for all other pans). Spray 15x10x1-inch pan with cooking spray.

2 Unroll dough in pan; starting at center, press dough into 15x10-inch rectangle. Bake about 8 minutes or until light brown.

3 Meanwhile, in medium bowl, place chicken and barbecue sauce. Using 2 forks, toss until chicken is coated with sauce.

4 Sprinkle 1 cup of the cheese over partially baked crust. Spoon and spread chicken mixture evenly over cheese. Top with onion and remaining 1 cup cheese. Bake about 5 minutes or until cheese is melted. Cut into 6 rows by 3 rows. Sprinkle with parsley.

1 Serving: Calories 430; Total Fat 15g (Saturated Fat 6g, Trans Fat 0g); Cholesterol 60mg; Sodium 980mg; Total Carbohydrate 45g (Dietary Fiber 2g); Protein 30g **Exchanges:** 2 Starch, 1 Other Carbohydrate, 2 Very Lean Meat, 1½ Lean Meat, 1½ Fat **Carbohydrate Choices:** 3

Easy Success Tip

You can use leftover cut-up cooked chicken breast, or pick up a rotisserie chicken at the supermarket. Remove the chicken from the bones, and cut into bite-size pieces.

gluten-free chicken pesto pizza

prep time: 10 Minutes • **start to finish:** 30 Minutes • 6 servings

1 container Pillsbury Gluten Free refrigerated pizza crust dough

⅓ cup refrigerated gluten-free basil pesto

1 cup shredded mozzarella cheese or gluten-free Italian cheese blend (4 oz)

1 cup diced cooked chicken

1 large plum (Roma) tomato, thinly sliced

Thinly sliced fresh basil leaves, if desired

1 Heat oven to 400°F. Grease cookie sheet and hands. Press dough into 11-inch round on cookie sheet.

2 Bake 12 to 14 minutes or until edge is beginning to brown. Spread pesto to within ½ inch of edge of partially baked crust. Top with ½ cup of the cheese, the chicken and tomato; sprinkle with remaining ½ cup cheese.

3 Bake 8 to 10 minutes or until crust is deep golden brown and cheese is melted. Sprinkle with basil.

1 Serving: Calories 200; Total Fat 14g (Saturated Fat 4g, Trans Fat 0g); Cholesterol 35mg; Sodium 350mg; Total Carbohydrate 7g (Dietary Fiber 0g); Protein 13g **Exchanges:** ½ Starch, ½ Very Lean Meat, ½ Lean Meat, ½ Medium-Fat Meat, 2 Fat **Carbohydrate Choices:** ½

Easy Success Tips

You may want to try gluten-free sun-dried tomato pesto instead of the basil pesto for a nice flavor change.

If you are cooking gluten free, always read labels to make sure each recipe ingredient is gluten free. Products and ingredient sources can change.

chicken pesto pizza

prep time: 15 Minutes • start to finish: 25 Minutes • 6 servings (3 pieces each)

1 can Pillsbury refrigerated artisan pizza crust with whole grain

½ cup refrigerated basil pesto (from 7-oz container)

2 cups shredded reduced-fat mozzarella cheese or Italian cheese blend (8 oz)

1 cup shredded cooked chicken breast

2 large plum (Roma) tomatoes, thinly sliced

Fresh basil leaves, if desired

1 Heat oven to 400°F for dark or nonstick pan (425°F for all other pans). Spray 15x10x1-inch pan with cooking spray.

2 Unroll dough in pan; starting at center, press dough into 15x10-inch rectangle. Bake about 8 minutes or until light brown.

3 Spread pesto to within ½ inch of edges of partially baked crust. Top with 1½ cups of the cheese, the chicken and tomatoes; sprinkle with remaining ½ cup cheese.

4 Bake 5 minutes or until edges of crust are golden brown and cheese is melted. Sprinkle with basil. Cut into 6 rows by 3 rows.

1 Serving: Calories 450; Total Fat 25g (Saturated Fat 8g, Trans Fat 0g); Cholesterol 45mg; Sodium 800mg; Total Carbohydrate 33g (Dietary Fiber 2g); Protein 25g **Exchanges:** 1½ Starch, ½ Other Carbohydrate, 1 Very Lean Meat, 2 Lean Meat, 3½ Fat **Carbohydrate Choices:** 2

Easy Success Tips

For an appetizer, cut the pizza into bite-size squares, and insert a party toothpick into each piece.

Go from turf to surf! Use ½ pound cooked shrimp in place of the chicken in this recipe.

gluten-free chicken alfredo pizza

prep time: 15 Minutes • start to finish: 25 Minutes • 6 servings

1 container Pillsbury Gluten Free refrigerated pizza crust dough

¾ cup gluten-free Alfredo pasta sauce (from 15-oz jar)

2 cups chopped cooked chicken

1½ cups packed fresh baby spinach leaves

1 cup gluten-free shredded Italian cheese blend or mozzarella cheese (4 oz)

1 Heat oven to 400°F. Grease cookie sheet and hands. Press dough into 12x10-inch rectangle on cookie sheet.

2 Bake 10 to 12 minutes or until edges are beginning to brown. Meanwhile, in medium bowl, mix Alfredo sauce and chicken; spoon evenly over partially baked crust. Top with spinach and cheese.

3 Bake 8 to 10 minutes or until crust is deep golden brown and cheese is melted. Cool 5 minutes before serving.

1 Serving: Calories 280; Total Fat 18g (Saturated Fat 10g, Trans Fat 0.5g); Cholesterol 85mg; Sodium 400mg; Total Carbohydrate 8g (Dietary Fiber 0g); Protein 20g **Exchanges:** ½ Starch, 1 Very Lean Meat, 1 Lean Meat, ½ High-Fat Meat, 2 Fat **Carbohydrate Choices:** ½

Easy Success Tips

Add ½ cup thinly sliced mushrooms to the pizza when topping with the spinach.

If you are cooking gluten free, always read labels to make sure each recipe ingredient is gluten free. Products and ingredient sources can change.

sweet chicken and gouda pizza

prep time: 15 Minutes • start to finish: 25 Minutes • 6 servings

1 can Pillsbury refrigerated thin pizza crust

½ cup peach-apricot preserves

½ teaspoon dried thyme leaves

½ teaspoon salt

½ teaspoon pepper

1 cup chopped deli rotisserie chicken breast

⅓ cup cooked real bacon pieces (from 2.8-oz package)

7 oz Gouda cheese, shredded (1¾ cups)

1 Heat oven to 425°F. Brush 15x10x1-inch nonstick or dark pan with vegetable oil. Unroll dough in pan. Starting at center, press out dough to edge of pan. Bake about 6 minutes or until light golden brown.

2 Meanwhile, in small bowl, stir preserves, thyme, salt and pepper until well blended.

3 Spread preserves mixture over partially baked crust. Top with chicken, bacon and cheese. Bake 8 to 10 minutes or until cheese is melted and edges are golden brown.

1 Serving: Calories 410; Total Fat 19g (Saturated Fat 8g, Trans Fat 0g); Cholesterol 65mg; Sodium 800mg; Total Carbohydrate 42g (Dietary Fiber 1g); Protein 19g **Exchanges:** 2 Starch, 1 Low-Fat Milk, ½ Lean Meat, 2½ Fat **Carbohydrate Choices:** 3

apricot-dijon chicken and arugula pizza

prep time: 20 Minutes • **start to finish:** 30 Minutes • 8 servings

1 can Pillsbury refrigerated thin pizza crust

½ cup apricot preserves

1 tablespoon whole-grain or country-style Dijon mustard

2 cups coarsely chopped deli rotisserie chicken

7 slices precooked bacon, chopped

3 cups shredded Gruyère cheese (12 oz)

2 cups arugula

1 Heat oven to 400°F. Spray large dark cookie sheet with cooking spray. Unroll dough on cookie sheet. Bake 8 minutes.

2 Meanwhile, in small microwavable bowl, stir preserves and mustard until well blended. Microwave uncovered on High 20 to 30 seconds or until melted.

3 Sprinkle chicken over partially baked crust. Drizzle with mustard mixture. Top with bacon, 1½ cups of the cheese, the arugula and remaining 1½ cups cheese.

4 Bake 8 to 10 minutes or until cheese is melted.

1 Serving: Calories 430; Total Fat 22g (Saturated Fat 10g, Trans Fat 0g); Cholesterol 85mg; Sodium 680mg; Total Carbohydrate 32g (Dietary Fiber 0g); Protein 28g **Exchanges:** 1 Starch, 1 Other Carbohydrate, 2 Lean Meat, 1½ Medium-Fat Meat, 1½ Fat **Carbohydrate Choices:** 2

naan greek pizzas

prep time: 20 Minutes • **start to finish:** 35 Minutes • 8 pizzas

1 can (16.3 oz) Pillsbury Grands! Homestyle refrigerated buttermilk biscuits (8 biscuits)

2 tablespoons garlic-infused olive oil or olive oil

1 box (9 oz) frozen chopped spinach

2 cups shredded or diced cooked chicken

3 tablespoons Greek seasoning mix

1 cup tzatziki

4 oz crumbled feta cheese (1 cup)

1 Heat oven to 400°F. Separate dough into 8 biscuits. To make naan, place biscuits between layers of waxed paper; roll into 8x6-inch ovals. Brush ovals with 1 tablespoon of the oil. Place on ungreased large cookie sheets, oil side down; brush tops with remaining oil. Bake 7 to 13 minutes or until golden brown.

2 Meanwhile, microwave frozen spinach as directed on box. In large bowl, mix spinach, chicken and 2 tablespoons of the seasoning mix.

3 Spread 2 tablespoons tzatziki on each naan. Top with chicken mixture, cheese and remaining seasoning mix. Bake 2 to 3 minutes or until thoroughly heated.

1 Pizza: Calories 340; Total Fat 17g (Saturated Fat 7g, Trans Fat 0g); Cholesterol 45mg; Sodium 1190mg; Total Carbohydrate 28g (Dietary Fiber 1g); Protein 16g **Exchanges:** 2 Starch, 1 Very Lean Meat, ½ Medium-Fat Meat, 2½ Fat **Carbohydrate Choices:** 2

Easy Success Tips

Some Greek seasonings contain a high amount of salt. For best results, look for a Greek seasoning with dried herbs in your grocery store.

Tzatziki is a yogurt cucumber sauce. Look for it in the dairy section of your grocery store.

taco pizza

prep time: 20 Minutes • start to finish: 30 Minutes • 6 servings (3 pieces each)

3 links (4 oz each) spicy Italian turkey sausage, casings removed, crumbled

½ cup canned enchilada sauce

1 can Pillsbury refrigerated artisan pizza crust with whole grain

2 cups shredded Mexican cheese blend (8 oz)

2 medium plum (Roma) tomatoes, chopped

1 medium yellow bell pepper, chopped (1 cup), if desired

¼ cup chopped fresh cilantro or green onions, if desired

1 Heat oven to 400°F for dark or nonstick pan (425°F for all other pans). Spray 15x10x1-inch pan with cooking spray.

2 In 12-inch skillet, cook sausage over medium heat, stirring occasionally to crumble sausage, until no longer pink; drain and remove from skillet. Gently stir enchilada sauce into sausage to coat.

3 Unroll dough in pan; starting at center, press dough into 15x10-inch rectangle. Bake about 8 minutes or until light brown.

4 Spoon and spread sausage mixture over partially baked crust. Sprinkle with 1½ cups of the cheese. Top with tomatoes and bell pepper; sprinkle with remaining ½ cup cheese.

5 Bake 8 to 10 minutes or until crust is golden brown and cheese is melted. Garnish with cilantro. Cut into 6 rows by 3 rows.

1 Serving: Calories 420; Total Fat 21g (Saturated Fat 9g, Trans Fat 0g); Cholesterol 65mg; Sodium 1060mg; Total Carbohydrate 33g (Dietary Fiber 2g); Protein 23g **Exchanges:** 2 Starch, ½ Vegetable, 1½ Lean Meat, 1 Medium-Fat Meat, 2 Fat **Carbohydrate Choices:** 2

Easy Success Tips

Control the heat in this pizza by selecting mild, medium or hot enchilada sauce.

Turkey sausage is low in fat but high in flavor! Check the label on the sausage to make sure it is made with turkey breast, which is lower in fat than turkey sausage made with dark meat.

philly cheese steak pizza

prep time: 30 Minutes • **start to finish:** 50 Minutes • 6 servings (3 pieces each)

2 teaspoons olive oil

1 large sweet onion, sliced (1 cup)

1 can Pillsbury refrigerated artisan pizza crust with whole grain

½ cup pizza sauce

⅓ lb deli-style roast beef, roughly chopped

2 cups shredded provolone cheese (8 oz)

¾ cup sliced green bell pepper

1 Heat oven to 400°F for dark or nonstick pan (425°F for all other pans). Spray 15x10x1-inch pan with cooking spray.

2 In 12-inch nonstick skillet, heat oil over medium-high heat. Stir in onion to coat with oil. Cook uncovered 10 minutes, stirring every 3 to 4 minutes. Reduce heat to medium-low. Cook about 20 minutes longer, stirring well every 5 minutes, until onions are golden brown (onions will shrink during cooking). Set aside.

3 Unroll dough in pan; starting at center, press dough into 15x10-inch rectangle. Bake about 8 minutes or until light brown.

4 Spread pizza sauce over partially baked crust. Top with roast beef, onion, cheese and bell pepper.

5 Bake 8 to 10 minutes or until crust is golden brown and cheese is melted. Cut into 6 rows by 3 rows

1 Serving: Calories 390; Total Fat 18g (Saturated Fat 8g, Trans Fat 0g); Cholesterol 40mg; Sodium 1000mg; Total Carbohydrate 36g (Dietary Fiber 3g); Protein 21g **Exchanges:** 1½ Starch, ½ Other Carbohydrate, 1 Vegetable, 1 Lean Meat, 1 Medium-Fat Meat, 2 Fat **Carbohydrate Choices:** 2½

Easy Success Tips

The Philly cheese steak sandwich originated in Philadelphia in the 1930s. Thinly sliced beef is layered on a French or Italian roll and topped with American cheese and sautéed onions. The classic has been modified to include other cheese varieties such as Cheddar or provolone.

In place of the regular roast beef, try Cajun- or Italian-seasoned roast beef from the deli. Or if you prefer, use sliced cooked turkey.

gluten-free bacon cheeseburger pizza

prep time: 10 Minutes • **start to finish:** 40 Minutes • 6 servings

1 container Pillsbury Gluten Free refrigerated pizza crust dough

1 lb lean (at least 80%) ground beef, cooked, drained

1 can (8 oz) gluten-free pizza sauce

4 slices gluten-free bacon, crisply cooked, coarsely chopped

1 cup shredded Cheddar cheese (4 oz)

Shredded lettuce, sliced tomatoes and/or pickle slices, if desired

1 Heat oven to 400°F. Grease cookie sheet and hands. Press dough into 11-inch round on cookie sheet.

2 Bake 12 to 14 minutes or until edge is beginning to brown. Meanwhile, in medium bowl, mix cooked beef and pizza sauce. Spread on partially baked crust to within ½ inch of edge. Top with bacon and cheese.

3 Bake 8 to 10 minutes or until crust is deep golden brown and cheese is melted. Top with lettuce, tomatoes and pickles. Cool 5 minutes before serving.

1 Serving: Calories 280; Total Fat 18g (Saturated Fat 8g, Trans Fat 1g); Cholesterol 75mg; Sodium 440mg; Total Carbohydrate 9g (Dietary Fiber 1g); Protein 21g **Exchanges:** ½ Starch, 2 Lean Meat, ½ High-Fat Meat, 1½ Fat **Carbohydrate Choices:** ½

Easy Success Tips

What are your favorite cheeseburger toppings? Top this tasty gluten-free pizza with the toppings you like best—whether pickle slices or relish, ketchup or mustard—make it your own way!

If you are cooking gluten free, always read labels to make sure each recipe ingredient is gluten free. Products and ingredient sources can change.

gluten-free sloppy joe pizza

prep time: 10 Minutes • start to finish: 35 Minutes • 6 servings

1 container Pillsbury Gluten Free refrigerated pizza crust dough

1 lb lean (at least 80%) ground beef, cooked, drained

1 can (15½ oz) gluten-free original sloppy joe sauce

1 cup shredded Cheddar cheese (4 oz)

2 medium green onions, sliced (2 tablespoons)

1 Heat oven to 400°F. Grease cookie sheet and hands. Press dough into 12x10-inch rectangle on cookie sheet.

2 Bake 12 to 14 minutes or until edge is beginning to brown. Meanwhile, in 10-inch skillet, cook beef and sloppy joe sauce over medium heat, stirring occasionally, until hot. Spoon beef mixture over partially baked crust. Sprinkle with cheese.

3 Bake 8 to 10 minutes or until crust is deep golden brown and cheese is melted. Sprinkle with green onions. Let stand 5 minutes before serving.

1 Serving: Calories 270; Total Fat 15g (Saturated Fat 7g, Trans Fat 0.5g); Cholesterol 65mg; Sodium 690mg; Total Carbohydrate 12g (Dietary Fiber 1g); Protein 19g **Exchanges:** ½ Starch, ½ Other Carbohydrate, 2 Lean Meat, ½ High-Fat Meat, 1 Fat **Carbohydrate Choices:** 1

Easy Success Tips

Kick up the flavor by adding ¼ teaspoon ground red pepper (cayenne) to the meat mixture, and top with gluten-free shredded pepper Jack cheese instead of the Cheddar.

If you are cooking gluten free, always read labels to make sure each recipe ingredient is gluten free. Products and ingredient sources can change.

breakfast pizza

prep time: 30 Minutes • start to finish: 30 Minutes • 6 servings

1 can Pillsbury refrigerated artisan pizza crust with whole grain

½ cup coarsely chopped bacon

6 eggs, beaten

4 oz (half of 8-oz package) cream cheese, cut into small pieces

2 cups shredded Monterey Jack cheese with jalapeño peppers (8 oz)

½ cup sliced red bell pepper

¼ cup thinly sliced red onion

Fresh chopped cilantro, if desired

Salsa, if desired

1 Heat oven to 400°F for dark or nonstick pan (425°F for all other pans). Spray 14-inch round pizza pan with cooking spray.

2 Unroll dough on pan. Starting at center, press out dough to edge of pan. Bake about 8 minutes or until crust edge begins to set.

3 Meanwhile, in 10-inch skillet, cook bacon 4 to 6 minutes over medium-high heat or until just crispy, stirring frequently. Remove bacon; drain drippings, leaving 1 teaspoon in skillet.

4 In same skillet, add eggs; cook 2 to 3 minutes, stirring frequently, until firm but still moist.

5 Spoon and spread eggs over partially baked crust. Scatter cream cheese over eggs. Top with Monterey Jack cheese, bell pepper, onion and bacon. Bake 9 to 13 minutes or until crust is golden brown and cheese is melted. Cut into 6 wedges. Sprinkle with cilantro, and serve with salsa.

1 Serving: Calories 490; Total Fat 29g (Saturated Fat 14g, Trans Fat 0g); Cholesterol 245mg; Sodium 760mg; Total Carbohydrate 33g (Dietary Fiber 2g); Protein 23g **Exchanges:** 2 Starch, 2½ Medium-Fat Meat, 3 Fat **Carbohydrate Choices:** 2

Easy Success Tips

You can use plain Monterey Jack or Cheddar cheese in place of pepper Jack. And you can use flavored cream cheese in place of the plain cream cheese.

If you do not have a round pizza pan, just press the crust into a 15x10x1-inch pan sprayed with cooking spray.

gluten-free personal pepperoni pizzas

prep time: **10 Minutes** • start to finish: **30 Minutes** • **6 pizzas**

1 container Pillsbury Gluten Free refrigerated pizza crust dough

¾ cup gluten-free pizza sauce

1 cup shredded mozzarella cheese (4 oz)

30 slices gluten-free pepperoni (about 2 oz)

1 Heat oven to 400°F. Grease 2 cookie sheets and hands. Divide dough into 6 pieces; press each into 6-inch round. Place 3 rounds on each cookie sheet.

2 Bake 8 minutes. Top partially baked crusts with remaining ingredients.

3 Bake 6 to 9 minutes or until crusts are deep golden brown and cheese is melted.

1 Pizza: Calories 150; Total Fat 9g (Saturated Fat 3.5g, Trans Fat 0g); Cholesterol 20mg; Sodium 440mg; Total Carbohydrate 8g (Dietary Fiber 1g); Protein 8g **Exchanges:** ½ Starch, 1 Medium-Fat Meat, ½ Fat **Carbohydrate Choices:** ½

Easy Success Tips

Customize your pizzas by adding ingredients such as chopped tomato, green bell pepper or mushrooms before topping with cheese.

If you are cooking gluten free, always read labels to make sure each recipe ingredient is gluten free. Products and ingredient sources can change.

gluten-free mexican breakfast pizza

prep time: **25 Minutes** • start to finish: **35 Minutes** • **6 servings**

1 container Pillsbury Gluten Free refrigerated pizza crust dough

½ lb gluten-free chorizo or bulk spicy Italian pork sausage

4 eggs, beaten

1 cup gluten-free salsa

1 cup shredded Monterey Jack cheese (4 oz)

Chopped fresh cilantro, if desired

1 Heat oven to 400°F. Grease cookie sheet and hands. Press dough into 11-inch round on cookie sheet.

2 Bake 12 to 14 minutes or until edge is beginning to brown.

3 Meanwhile, in 10-inch nonstick skillet, cook and stir chorizo over medium-high heat until no longer pink. Drain; remove to small bowl. Wipe out skillet. Add eggs to skillet; cook over medium-low heat until almost set. Stir in chorizo. Spread ½ cup of the salsa over partially baked crust. Spoon egg mixture over salsa, covering crust completely. Sprinkle with cheese.

4 Bake 8 to 10 minutes or until crust is deep golden brown and cheese is melted. Sprinkle with cilantro. Serve with remaining ½ cup salsa.

1 Serving: Calories 330; Total Fat 25g (Saturated Fat 10g, Trans Fat 0g); Cholesterol 175mg; Sodium 970mg; Total Carbohydrate 9g (Dietary Fiber 1g); Protein 19g
Exchanges: ½ Starch, 1 Medium-Fat Meat, 1½ High-Fat Meat, 1½ Fat **Carbohydrate Choices:** ½

Easy Success Tips

Breakfast pizza also makes a great weeknight supper. Offer additional toppings, such as gluten-free sour cream, guacamole or chopped avocado to make it special!

If you are cooking gluten free, always read labels to make sure each recipe ingredient is gluten free. Products and ingredient sources can change.

sweet pulled pork pizza

prep time: 25 Minutes • start to finish: 40 Minutes • 8 servings

1 can Pillsbury refrigerated thin pizza crust

1 package (12 oz) fully cooked sauceless hickory-smoked seasoned pulled pork

½ cup peach-apricot preserves

4 oz blue cheese, crumbled (1 cup)

8 oz extra-sharp white Cheddar cheese, shredded (2 cups)

½ cup finely chopped red onion

¼ cup chopped walnuts

1 Heat oven to 400°F. Spray 15x10x1-inch pan with cooking spray. Unroll dough in pan; prick dough several times with fork. Bake 8 minutes.

2 Heat pork in microwave as directed on package; set aside.

3 Spread preserves over partially baked crust to within ½ inch of edges. Top with pork, blue cheese, Cheddar cheese and onion.

4 Bake 8 minutes. Top with walnuts. Bake 5 minutes longer or until crust is golden brown and cheese is melted.

1 Serving: Calories 450; Total Fat 26g (Saturated Fat 12g, Trans Fat 0g); Cholesterol 65mg; Sodium 840mg; Total Carbohydrate 32g (Dietary Fiber 1g); Protein 21g **Exchanges:** 1 Starch, 1 Other Carbohydrate, 1 Very Lean Meat, ½ Medium-Fat Meat, 1 High-Fat Meat, 3 Fat **Carbohydrate Choices:** 2

ham and creamy sriracha pizza

prep time: 20 Minutes • **start to finish:** 30 Minutes • 6 servings

¼ cup peach-apricot preserves

2 packages (3 oz each) cream cheese, softened

3 tablespoons Sriracha sauce

4 cloves garlic, crushed or finely chopped (about 2 teaspoons)

1 can Pillsbury refrigerated classic pizza crust

8 oz sliced deli ham, cut into 1-inch pieces

½ cup fresh cilantro, chopped

1 Heat oven to 400°F. Grease large cookie sheet.

2 In small bowl, mix preserves, cream cheese, Sriracha sauce and garlic until well blended.

3 Unroll dough on cookie sheet; press dough into 15x10-inch rectangle. Bake 8 minutes. Spread cream cheese mixture over partially baked crust; top with ham.

4 Bake 6 to 10 minutes or until crust is golden brown. Sprinkle with cilantro.

1 Serving: Calories 360; Total Fat 14g (Saturated Fat 7g, Trans Fat 0g); Cholesterol 50mg; Sodium 1170mg; Total Carbohydrate 44g (Dietary Fiber 1g); Protein 15g **Exchanges:** 1½ Starch, 1½ Other Carbohydrate, 1½ Medium-Fat Meat, 1 Fat **Carbohydrate Choices:** 3

caramelized onion polish pizza

prep time: 25 Minutes • **start to finish:** 40 Minutes • 6 servings

1 **can Pillsbury refrigerated classic pizza crust**

2 **teaspoons caraway seed**

1 **tablespoon olive oil**

2 **large sweet onions, cut in half, thinly sliced**

1 **package (14 oz) fully cooked Polska kielbasa, cut in half lengthwise, thinly sliced**

1 **cup sauerkraut, well drained**

12 **slices Swiss cheese (9 oz)**

1 Heat oven to 400°F. Place oven rack in lower one-third of oven. Spray 15x10x1-inch pan with cooking spray. Unroll dough in pan; press in bottom and halfway up sides. Sprinkle 1 teaspoon of the caraway seed over dough. Bake 12 to 15 minutes or until crust is light golden brown.

2 Meanwhile, in 4-quart saucepan or Dutch oven, heat oil over medium-high heat. Add onions; cook 8 to 10 minutes, stirring frequently, until onions start to caramelize. Add kielbasa; cook 10 minutes, stirring frequently, until mixture is golden brown and caramelized. Stir in sauerkraut.

3 Spread kielbasa mixture over partially baked crust. Top with cheese. Sprinkle with remaining 1 teaspoon caraway seed. Bake 10 to 12 minutes or until crust is deep golden brown and cheese is melted.

1 Serving: Calories 580; Total Fat 35g (Saturated Fat 15g, Trans Fat 1g); Cholesterol 80mg; Sodium 1430mg; Total Carbohydrate 42g (Dietary Fiber 3g); Protein 25g **Exchanges:** 1½ Starch, 1½ Other Carbohydrate, 1 Medium-Fat Meat, 2 High-Fat Meat, 2½ Fat **Carbohydrate Choices:** 3

gluten-free chicago deep-dish pizza

prep time: 25 Minutes • start to finish: 45 Minutes • 6 servings

1 container Pillsbury Gluten Free refrigerated pizza crust dough

12 oz gluten-free bulk Italian pork sausage

¾ cup chopped green bell pepper

1 cup sliced fresh mushrooms

1 can (8 oz) gluten-free pizza sauce

1 cup shredded mozzarella cheese (4 oz)

2 medium plum (Roma) tomatoes, chopped

1 Heat oven to 400°F. Grease 9-inch round cake pan and hands. Press dough in bottom and all the way up side of pan.

2 Bake 12 to 14 minutes or until edge is beginning to brown. Meanwhile, in 10-inch nonstick skillet, cook sausage and ½ cup of the bell pepper 7 to 9 minutes, stirring frequently, until sausage is no longer pink; drain. Stir in mushrooms and pizza sauce. Keep warm over low heat.

3 Spread ½ cup of the cheese evenly in bottom of partially baked crust. Spoon hot sausage mixture over cheese. Top with remaining ½ cup cheese, the tomatoes and remaining ¼ cup bell pepper.

4 Bake 8 to 10 minutes or until crust is deep golden brown and cheese is melted. Let stand 5 minutes before serving.

1 Serving: Calories 260; Total Fat 16g (Saturated Fat 6g, Trans Fat 0g); Cholesterol 35mg; Sodium 790mg; Total Carbohydrate 13g (Dietary Fiber 2g); Protein 14g **Exchanges:** ½ Starch, 1 Vegetable, ½ Medium-Fat Meat, 1 High-Fat Meat, 1 Fat **Carbohydrate Choices:** 1

Easy Success Tips

Pass the grated gluten-free Parmesan cheese and crushed red pepper—no Chicago-style pizza is complete without them!

If you are cooking gluten free, always read labels to make sure each recipe ingredient is gluten free. Products and ingredient sources can change.

smoky chorizo pizza

prep time: **25 Minutes** • start to finish: **35 Minutes** • **6 servings**

1 tablespoon plus 1½ teaspoons olive oil

1 can Pillsbury refrigerated classic pizza crust

5 oz cooked smoked Spanish chorizo, coarsely chopped

1 medium sweet onion, cut in half, thinly sliced (2 cups)

2 tablespoons sherry vinegar

12 oz sliced provolone cheese

½ cup sliced roasted red bell pepper (from 7-oz jar), drained

1 Heat oven to 400°F. Brush 1½ teaspoons of the oil on large cookie sheet. Unroll dough on cookie sheet; press into 14x12-inch rectangle. Brush remaining 1 tablespoon oil over dough. Bake 8 minutes.

2 Meanwhile, heat 10-inch nonstick skillet over medium-high heat. Add chorizo; cook 4 to 5 minutes, stirring occasionally, until meat starts to brown. Drain on paper towels. Reduce heat to medium. Add onion; cook 5 minutes, stirring occasionally. Stir in vinegar; cook 5 minutes longer or until onion is soft and caramelized. Remove from heat.

3 Top partially baked crust with cheese, onion, roasted pepper and chorizo. Bake 8 to 10 minutes or until crust is golden brown and cheese is bubbly.

1 Serving: Calories 520; Total Fat 30g (Saturated Fat 14g, Trans Fat 0g); Cholesterol 60mg; Sodium 1280mg; Total Carbohydrate 39g (Dietary Fiber 2g); Protein 25g **Exchanges:** 1½ Starch, 1½ Low-Fat Milk, 1 Medium-Fat Meat, 3 Fat **Carbohydrate Choices:** 2½

gluten-free veggie pizza

prep time: 10 Minutes • start to finish: 40 Minutes • 6 servings

1 container Pillsbury Gluten Free refrigerated pizza crust dough

½ cup gluten-free pizza sauce

½ medium bell pepper (any color), cut into thin strips

1 cup sliced mushrooms

1 cup shredded mozzarella cheese (4 oz)

Thinly sliced fresh basil leaves, if desired

1 Heat oven to 400°F. Grease cookie sheet and hands. Press dough into 11-inch round on cookie sheet.

2 Bake 12 to 14 minutes or until edge is beginning to brown. Spread partially baked crust with pizza sauce to within ½ inch of edge. Top with bell pepper, mushrooms and cheese.

3 Bake 8 to 10 minutes or until crust is deep golden brown and cheese is melted. Top with basil leaves. Cool 5 minutes before serving.

1 Serving: Calories 100; Total Fat 5g (Saturated Fat 2g, Trans Fat 0g); Cholesterol 10mg; Sodium 260mg; Total Carbohydrate 8g (Dietary Fiber 1g); Protein 6g **Exchanges:** ½ Starch, ½ Vegetable, ½ Medium-Fat Meat, ½ Fat **Carbohydrate Choices:** ½

Easy Success Tips

Kick up the flavor a notch by sprinkling the pizza with crushed red pepper.

If you are cooking gluten free, always read labels to make sure each recipe ingredient is gluten free. Products and ingredient sources can change.

Gluten-Free Baking Tips

Our gluten-free refrigerated dough products offer the option to make pizzas, cookies and pies that are gluten free. For the best results, be sure to follow the directions on the package and in individual recipes. Here are some general gluten-free baking tips to help make your efforts a success.

- Store Pillsbury gluten-free dough products on the shelf in the refrigerator. Keep these products cold until just before using.

- For the best results with Pillsbury dough products, use by the expiration date on the package.

- Many foods are naturally gluten free. Shop the bounty of fresh fruits and vegetables for many gluten-free choices. Meat, poultry and fish are also naturally free of gluten.

- Always read labels of products that you use to make sure each recipe ingredient is gluten free.

- Keep a variety of gluten-free ingredients on hand.

- When cooking gluten free, it's important to keep things free from contact with gluten — sometimes called cross contamination. Keep the kitchen and all equipment that is used for gluten-free cooking very clean to eliminate this problem.

- Use separate utensils, pans, cutting board, etc. when you are gluten-free cooking. Color coding these items is a good way to keep the gluten-free equipment separate.

pear and gorgonzola pizza

prep time: 15 Minutes • start to finish: 30 Minutes • 6 servings (3 pieces each)

2 teaspoons olive oil

1 medium onion, chopped (½ cup)

1 firm ripe pear, cut in half, then cut into ¼-inch slices (1 cup)

1 can Pillsbury refrigerated artisan pizza crust with whole grain

6 oz provolone cheese, shredded (1½ cups)

¾ cup crumbled Gorgonzola cheese (3 oz)

2 cups loosely packed baby spinach

1 Heat oven to 400°F for dark or nonstick pan (425°F for all other pans). Spray 15x10x1-inch pan with cooking spray.

2 Heat 10-inch skillet over medium heat. Add oil and onion; cook about 5 minutes, stirring occasionally, until onion is softened and starting to brown. Reserve ½ cup pear. Stir remaining pear into onion. Cook 2 minutes, stirring frequently.

3 Unroll dough in pan; starting at center, press dough into 15x10-inch rectangle. Bake about 8 minutes or until light brown.

4 Top partially baked crust evenly with provolone cheese. Top with pear mixture and Gorgonzola cheese.

5 Bake 8 to 10 minutes or until crust is golden brown and cheese is melted. Top with spinach and reserved ½ cup pear slices. Cut into 6 rows by 3 rows.

1 Serving: Calories 380; Total Fat 18g (Saturated Fat 9g, Trans Fat 0g); Cholesterol 30mg; Sodium 830mg; Total Carbohydrate 38g (Dietary Fiber 3g); Protein 17g **Exchanges:** 2 Starch, ½ Other Carbohydrate, ½ Vegetable, ½ Lean Meat, 1 Medium-Fat Meat, 2 Fat **Carbohydrate Choices:** 2½

Easy Success Tips

Using Gorgonzola cheese here will help you cut down on fat but not on flavor. Gorgonzola has a strong and slightly pungent flavor, so you need only a small amount to make a big flavor impact.

If you are serving a crowd, cut into small squares, and this pizza can serve 24!

gluten-free tomato and mozzarella pizza

prep time: 10 Minutes • **start to finish:** 35 Minutes • 6 servings

1 container Pillsbury Gluten Free refrigerated pizza crust dough

½ cup gluten-free pizza sauce

1 cup shredded mozzarella cheese (4 oz)

1 medium plum (Roma) tomato, thinly sliced

¼ cup fresh basil leaves

1 Heat oven to 400°F. Grease cookie sheet and hands. Press dough into 11-inch round on cookie sheet.

2 Bake 12 to 14 minutes or until edge is beginning to brown. Spread partially baked crust with pizza sauce to within ½ inch of edge. Top with cheese and tomato.

3 Bake 8 to 10 minutes or until crust is deep golden brown and cheese is melted. Top with basil leaves. Cool 5 minutes before serving.

1 Serving: Calories 100; Total Fat 5g (Saturated Fat 2g, Trans Fat 0g); Cholesterol 10mg; Sodium 260mg; Total Carbohydrate 8g (Dietary Fiber 1g); Protein 6g **Exchanges:** ½ Starch, ½ Medium-Fat Meat, ½ Fat **Carbohydrate Choices:** ½

Easy Success Tips

Fresh basil adds a wonderful flavor to this pizza, but don't worry if you don't have any. You can sprinkle 1 teaspoon dried basil over the pizza sauce before adding the tomato slices.

If you are cooking gluten free, always read labels to make sure each recipe ingredient is gluten free. Products and ingredient sources can change.

roasted garlic and mushroom flatbread

prep time: 30 Minutes • **start to finish:** 45 Minutes • 6 servings

3 **heads garlic**

8 **tablespoons olive oil**

2 **packages (8 oz each) sliced fresh mushrooms**

1 **can (15 oz) cannellini beans, drained**

1 **can Pillsbury refrigerated thin pizza crust**

2 **cups shredded mozzarella cheese (8 oz)**

30 **leaves fresh sage, thinly sliced**

¼ **teaspoon salt**

¼ **teaspoon pepper**

1 Heat oven to 400°F. Cut thin slice from base of each head of garlic. Rub each head with 1 teaspoon of the oil. Wrap heads individually in foil. Bake 30 minutes; remove from oven. Cool 5 minutes. Separate and peel cloves, or squeeze flesh from skins; discard skins.

2 Meanwhile, in 12-inch skillet, heat 2 tablespoons of the oil over medium-high heat. Add 1 package of the mushrooms; cook 2 minutes without stirring. Cook 2 minutes longer, stirring occasionally; drain. Place in large bowl. Repeat with 2 more tablespoons of the oil and the remaining mushrooms.

3 Place beans and 2 tablespoons of the oil in food processor. Cover; process about 30 seconds or until smooth.

4 Grease large cookie sheet with remaining 1 tablespoon oil. Unroll dough on cookie sheet. Press edges of dough with fork to create decorative border. Bake 6 minutes; remove from oven. Spread beans over partially baked crust to within ½ inch of edges. Sprinkle with cheese. Top with sage, mushrooms (drain, if necessary) and roasted garlic. Sprinkle with salt and pepper.

5 Bake about 10 minutes or until golden brown.

1 Serving: Calories 550; Total Fat 30g (Saturated Fat 8g, Trans Fat 0g); Cholesterol 20mg; Sodium 770mg; Total Carbohydrate 46g (Dietary Fiber 6g); Protein 23g **Exchanges:** 2½ Starch, 1½ Vegetable, 2 Lean Meat, 4½ Fat **Carbohydrate Choices:** 3

potato pesto pizza

prep time: 15 Minutes • **start to finish:** 25 Minutes • 6 servings (3 pieces each)

1 can Pillsbury refrigerated artisan pizza crust with whole grain

½ cup refrigerated basil pesto (from 7-oz container)

1 tablespoon chopped roasted garlic (from 4-oz jar)

2 cups shredded reduced-fat mozzarella cheese (8 oz)

4 small red potatoes, very thinly sliced (8 oz)

2 tablespoons sliced green onions (2 medium), if desired

1 Heat oven to 400°F for dark or nonstick pan (425°F for all other pans). Spray 15x10x1-inch pan with cooking spray.

2 Unroll dough in pan; starting at center, press dough into 15x10-inch rectangle. Bake 4 to 6 minutes or until edges begin to set.

3 In small bowl, stir 6 tablespoons of the pesto with the garlic. Spread over partially baked crust. Sprinkle with cheese. Top with potato slices, and brush remaining 2 tablespoons pesto over potatoes.

4 Bake 8 to 10 minutes or until crust is golden brown and cheese is melted. Garnish with green onions. Cut into 6 rows by 3 rows.

1 Serving: Calories 440; Total Fat 24g (Saturated Fat 7g, Trans Fat 0g); Cholesterol 25mg; Sodium 790mg; Total Carbohydrate 39g (Dietary Fiber 3g); Protein 18g **Exchanges:** 2½ Starch, 1½ Lean Meat, 3½ Fat **Carbohydrate Choices:** 2½

Easy Success Tips

Chopped roasted garlic in water, available in jars, is a great convenience item to keep on hand. You can also use fresh garlic, or roast your own.

Use purchased pesto, found near the refrigerated pasta in your supermarket.

gluten-free black bean salsa pizzas

prep time: **10 Minutes** • start to finish: **30 Minutes** • **6 pizzas**

1 container Pillsbury Gluten Free refrigerated pizza crust dough

1 can (15 oz) black beans, drained, rinsed

¾ cup gluten-free salsa

1½ cups gluten-free shredded Mexican cheese blend or Colby–Monterey Jack cheese blend (6 oz)

2 medium green onions, sliced (2 tablespoons)

1 Heat oven to 400°F. Grease 2 cookie sheets and hands. Divide dough into 6 pieces; press each into 6-inch round. Place 3 rounds on each cookie sheet.

2 Bake 8 minutes. In bowl, mix beans and salsa. Top partially baked crusts with bean mixture and cheese.

3 Bake 6 to 9 minutes or until crusts are deep golden brown and cheese is melted. Sprinkle with green onions.

1 Pizza: Calories 220; Total Fat 10g (Saturated Fat 6g, Trans Fat 0g); Cholesterol 30mg; Sodium 670mg; Total Carbohydrate 22g (Dietary Fiber 6g); Protein 12g **Exchanges:** 1½ Other Carbohydrate, ½ Vegetable, 1 Very Lean Meat, ½ High-Fat Meat, 1 Fat **Carbohydrate Choices:** 1½

Easy Success Tips

Try a chicken and black bean pizza—add about a cup of shredded cooked chicken to the black bean mixture.

If you are cooking gluten free, always read labels to make sure each recipe ingredient is gluten free. Products and ingredient sources can change.

thai shrimp pizza

prep time: 20 Minutes • start to finish: 30 Minutes • 6 servings

1 can Pillsbury refrigerated thin pizza crust

10 oz uncooked deveined peeled medium shrimp, thawed if frozen, tail shells removed

¾ cup crunchy peanut butter

¼ cup orange marmalade

2 tablespoons Thai chili garlic paste

¼ cup hot water

2 cups shredded Italian cheese blend (8 oz)

½ cup chopped fresh cilantro

1 Heat oven to 425°F. Spray large cookie sheet with cooking spray. Unroll dough on cookie sheet; press into 16½x11½-inch rectangle. Bake 5 minutes.

2 Meanwhile, cut shrimp in half; place in medium bowl. In small bowl, beat peanut butter, marmalade, chili garlic paste and hot water with whisk until thoroughly blended. Add 2 tablespoons of the peanut butter mixture to shrimp; stir thoroughly to coat. Spread remaining peanut butter mixture over partially baked crust to within ¼ inch of edges. Top with cheese and shrimp mixture.

3 Bake 6 to 8 minutes or until cheese is melted and crust is deep golden brown. Remove from oven; sprinkle with cilantro.

1 Serving: Calories 550; Total Fat 30g (Saturated Fat 10g, Trans Fat 0g); Cholesterol 105mg; Sodium 1090mg; Total Carbohydrate 41g (Dietary Fiber 3g); Protein 29g **Exchanges:** ½ Starch, 2 Other Carbohydrate, 3 Very Lean Meat, 1 High-Fat Meat, 4 Fat **Carbohydrate Choices:** 3

Parmesan Crescent-Topped Chicken à la King (page 172)

casseroles and dinner pies

country chicken-bacon pot pie

prep time: **30 Minutes** • start to finish: **1 Hour 10 Minutes** • **4 servings**

6 slices bacon, cut into ½-inch pieces

1 lb boneless skinless chicken thighs, cut into 1-inch pieces

¼ teaspoon salt

¼ teaspoon pepper

1 large onion, cut into wedges

1½ cups frozen sliced carrots (from 16-oz bag), thawed

1 can (14.75 oz) cream-style sweet corn

½ cup chicken broth

2 tablespoons country-style Dijon mustard

1 Pillsbury refrigerated pie crust, softened as directed on box

1 tablespoon milk

¼ cup shredded Parmesan cheese (1 oz)

Chopped fresh parsley

1 Heat oven to 400°F. Grease 11x7-inch (2-quart) glass baking dish with shortening or cooking spray.

2 In 10-inch nonstick skillet, cook bacon until crisp; remove with slotted spoon to paper towels to drain. Discard all but 1 tablespoon drippings. Cook chicken, salt and pepper in drippings over medium-high heat 4 minutes. Reduce heat to medium. Add onion; cook about 5 minutes or until onion is tender and chicken is no longer pink in center. Stir in carrots, corn, broth and mustard. Heat to boiling; boil 1 minute. Remove from heat. Stir in bacon. Spoon into baking dish.

3 Unroll pie crust on work surface. Cut into 1½-inch-wide strips. Place 4 strips crosswise over filling, trimming to fit. Place 3 longest strips lengthwise over filling. Brush strips with milk.

4 Bake 30 to 35 minutes or until crust is golden and filling is bubbly. Sprinkle cheese over crust. Bake 1 to 2 minutes longer or until cheese is melted. Sprinkle with parsley.

1 Serving: Calories 630; Total Fat 33g (Saturated Fat 13g, Trans Fat 0g); Cholesterol 105mg; Sodium 1550mg; Total Carbohydrate 48g (Dietary Fiber 3g); Protein 36g **Exchanges:** 2½ Starch, ½ Other Carbohydrate, ½ Vegetable, 4 Lean Meat, 4 Fat **Carbohydrate Choices:** 3

Easy Success Tip

Freeze leftover chicken broth in an ice cube tray. It will then be convenient to use any time you need just a little bit of broth.

chicken paprikash pot pie

prep time: 35 Minutes • **start to finish:** 1 Hour 20 Minutes • 6 servings

1 box Pillsbury refrigerated pie crusts, softened as directed on box

4 slices bacon, cut into ½-inch pieces

¾ lb boneless skinless chicken breasts, cut into ½-inch pieces

1 cup coarsely chopped onions

1 cup coarsely chopped red or green bell pepper

1 cup sliced carrots

1 cup frozen sweet peas

½ cup sour cream

1 jar (12 oz) home-style chicken gravy

3 tablespoons cornstarch

1 tablespoon paprika

1 Heat oven to 425°F. Make pie crust as directed on box for Two-Crust Pie using 9-inch pie plate.

2 In 10-inch skillet, cook bacon over medium heat until crisp. Reserve 1 tablespoon drippings with bacon in skillet, draining off remaining drippings.

3 Add chicken to skillet; cook and stir until no longer pink. Add onions, bell pepper and carrots; cook and stir until vegetables are tender. Stir in peas.

4 In small bowl, mix remaining ingredients. Stir into chicken mixture in skillet. Spoon into crust-lined pie plate. Top with second crust and flute edges; cut slits or small designs in several places on top of crust.

5 Bake 30 to 35 minutes or until crust is golden brown. Cover edge of crust with strips of foil after 10 to 15 minutes of baking to prevent excessive browning. Let stand 10 minutes before serving.

1 Serving: Calories 350; Total Fat 17g (Saturated Fat 7g, Trans Fat 0g); Cholesterol 55mg; Sodium 660mg; Total Carbohydrate 29g (Dietary Fiber 3g); Protein 19g **Exchanges:** 1½ Starch, 1 Vegetable, 2 Lean Meat, 2 Fat **Carbohydrate Choices:** 2

chicken and white bean bruschetta bake

prep time: 15 Minutes • **start to finish:** 45 Minutes • **4 servings (1½ cups each)**

1 can (19 oz) cannellini beans, drained, rinsed

1 can (14.5 oz) organic diced tomatoes with Italian herbs, drained

1 package (6 oz) refrigerated cooked Italian-flavor chicken breast strips, cut into 1-inch pieces

1 tablespoon balsamic vinegar

½ teaspoon salt

1 can Pillsbury refrigerated original breadsticks

2 cups shredded Italian cheese blend (8 oz)

½ teaspoon dried basil leaves, crushed

1 tablespoon chopped fresh parsley, if desired

1 Heat oven to 375°F. Spray 13x9-inch (3-quart) glass baking dish with cooking spray. In large bowl, mix beans, tomatoes, chicken, vinegar and salt.

2 Unroll dough; separate into 12 breadsticks. Cut each breadstick into 4 equal pieces. Stir one-fourth of breadstick pieces at a time into bean mixture. Stir in 1 cup of the cheese. Spoon into baking dish, gently smoothing top. Top evenly with remaining 1 cup cheese; sprinkle with basil.

3 Bake 25 to 30 minutes or until bubbly and top is golden brown. Spoon into 4 individual shallow soup bowls. Sprinkle with parsley.

1 Serving: Calories 630; Total Fat 20g (Saturated Fat 10g, Trans Fat 1g); Cholesterol 80mg; Sodium 1880mg; Total Carbohydrate 73g (Dietary Fiber 8g); Protein 40g **Exchanges:** 3½ Starch, 1 Other Carbohydrate, 1 Vegetable, 4 Very Lean Meat, 3 Fat **Carbohydrate Choices:** 5

gluten-free chicken pot pie

prep time: 15 Minutes • start to finish: 45 Minutes • 5 servings

1 can (18 oz) ready-to-serve creamy mushroom soup

1 bag (12 oz) frozen mixed vegetables

2 cups cubed cooked chicken

½ teaspoon garlic powder

¼ teaspoon dried thyme leaves

¼ cup gluten-free sour cream

½ container Pillsbury Gluten Free refrigerated pie and pastry dough

1 Heat oven to 425°F. In 2-quart saucepan, heat soup, vegetables, chicken, garlic powder and thyme to boiling. Remove from heat; stir in sour cream. Spoon into ungreased 2-quart casserole.

2 Knead dough until softened and no longer crumbly. Flatten into a round. Place between 2 sheets of cooking parchment or waxed paper. Roll into a round the size of casserole top. Carefully peel off top sheet of paper. Replace paper to cover loosely. Carefully turn dough over to remove second sheet of paper. Use paper to carefully turn dough over filling; remove paper. Press crust to edge of casserole. Cut slits in several places in crust.

3 Bake 20 to 25 minutes or until hot and bubbly and crust is golden brown. Let stand 5 minutes before serving.

1 Serving: Calories 620; Total Fat 37g (Saturated Fat 13g, Trans Fat 0g); Cholesterol 55mg; Sodium 960mg; Total Carbohydrate 51g (Dietary Fiber 2g); Protein 19g **Exchanges:** 1½ Starch, 1½ Other Carbohydrate, ½ Vegetable, 2 Very Lean Meat, 7 Fat **Carbohydrate Choices:** 3½

Easy Success Tips

To make individual chicken pot pies, pour mixture into 5 ungreased 10-oz custard cups or ramekins. Place on cookie sheet. Roll dough as directed, and cut into 5 (4½-inch) rounds, rerolling as needed. Place rounds over filling; press to sides of cups. Bake 15 to 25 minutes or until hot and bubbly and crust is golden brown.

If you are cooking gluten free, always read labels to make sure each recipe ingredient is gluten free. Products and ingredient sources can change.

chipotle chicken pie cups

prep time: **30 Minutes** • start to finish: **50 Minutes** • **8 servings**

2 cups coarsely chopped cooked chicken

⅔ cup chunky-style salsa

2 canned chipotle chiles in adobo sauce (with 2 tablespoons adobo sauce)

1 box Pillsbury refrigerated pie crusts, softened as directed on box

½ cup shredded Cheddar cheese (2 oz)

Lettuce, sour cream and guacamole, if desired

1 Heat oven to 400°F. Grease 8 regular-size muffin cups with shortening or cooking spray. Place chicken in medium bowl. In food processor, place salsa and chipotle chiles with adobo sauce. Cover; process until smooth. Add to chicken in bowl; stir.

2 Unroll pie crusts on work surface. Use 3½- to 4-inch round cutter to cut total of 8 rounds from pie crusts. Press rounds into muffin cups. Place chicken mixture in cups.

3 Bake 12 to 17 minutes or until filling is bubbly and pie crust is golden brown, topping with cheese during last 5 minutes of bake time. Cool 5 minutes; remove from muffin cups.

4 Serve with remaining ingredients.

1 Serving: Calories 280; Total Fat 16g (Saturated Fat 7g, Trans Fat 0g); Cholesterol 45mg; Sodium 470mg; Total Carbohydrate 23g (Dietary Fiber 0g); Protein 13g **Exchanges:** 1 Starch, ½ Other Carbohydrate, 1½ Very Lean Meat, 3 Fat **Carbohydrate Choices:** 1½

Easy Success Tips

To make pie pockets, heat oven to 400°F. Line cookie sheet with cooking parchment paper. Prepare chicken mixture as directed above. Cut each crust into quarters, making 8 wedges. Top half of each crust wedge with chicken mixture. Fold untopped sides of wedges over filling. With fork, press edges to seal. Place on cookie sheet. Cut several small slits in top of each to allow steam to escape. Bake 17 to 20 minutes or until edges are golden brown, topping with cheese during last 5 minutes of bake time. Remove from pan immediately. Serve with remaining ingredients.

For a milder flavor, omit the chipotle chiles in adobo sauce.

rustic chicken pot pies

prep time: 10 Minutes • start to finish: 35 Minutes • 4 servings

1 can (18.6 oz) ready-to-serve chicken pot pie–style soup

2 cups frozen mixed vegetables, thawed, drained

½ cup plain mashed potato flakes

½ teaspoon salt

¼ teaspoon pepper

1 box Pillsbury refrigerated pie crusts, softened as directed on box

2 cups prepared mashed potatoes

1 egg, beaten

1 Heat oven to 450°F. In 2-quart saucepan, heat soup, vegetables, dry potato mix, salt and pepper over medium heat until thickened.

2 Unroll pie crusts onto 2 ungreased cookie sheets. Spoon 1 cup mashed potatoes on center of each crust, spreading to within 2 inches of edge. Top with soup mixture, dividing evenly between crusts. Fold each crust over edge to form 2-inch border, pleating crust as necessary. Brush crusts with beaten egg.

3 Bake 20 to 25 minutes or until crust is golden brown.

1 Serving: Calories 670; Total Fat 33g (Saturated Fat 14g, Trans Fat 0g); Cholesterol 85mg; Sodium 1470mg; Total Carbohydrate 82g (Dietary Fiber 4g); Protein 12g **Exchanges:** 3 Starch, 2 Other Carbohydrate, 1 Vegetable, 6 Fat **Carbohydrate Choices:** 5½

mini crescent chicken pot pies

prep time: **15 Minutes** • start to finish: **30 Minutes** • **4 pot pies**

1½ cups frozen peas and carrots

1 cup cubed (½ inch) cooked chicken or turkey

1 cup refrigerated cooked diced potatoes with onions (from 20-oz bag)

¼ cup milk

½ teaspoon dried thyme leaves

1 can (10¾ oz) condensed cream of chicken soup

1 can (4 oz) Pillsbury refrigerated crescent dinner rolls (4 rolls)

1 egg

1 tablespoon water

⅛ teaspoon dried thyme leaves

1 Heat oven to 400°F. In 2-quart saucepan, mix peas and carrots, chicken, potatoes, milk, ½ teaspoon thyme and the soup. Heat to boiling over medium-high heat, stirring occasionally. Divide mixture evenly among 4 ungreased 10-oz custard cups.

2 Separate dough into 4 triangles. Place 1 dough triangle over each custard cup.

3 In small bowl, mix egg and water. Brush mixture over dough. Sprinkle ⅛ teaspoon thyme over dough. Bake 11 to 13 minutes or until crusts are golden brown.

1 Pot Pie: Calories 330; Total Fat 15g (Saturated Fat 5g, Trans Fat 1.5g); Cholesterol 90mg; Sodium 920mg; Total Carbohydrate 31g (Dietary Fiber 2g); Protein 18g **Exchanges:** 2 Starch, 1½ Lean Meat, 2 Fat **Carbohydrate Choices:** 2

Easy Success Tip

If you don't have 10-ounce custard cups, use foil tart pans (4½ inches in diameter by 1¼ inches tall). Look for them in the baking aisle of your grocery store.

crescent-topped hunter-style chicken

prep time: 25 Minutes • **start to finish:** 55 Minutes • 8 servings

1 tablespoon vegetable oil

1 cup ready-to-eat baby-cut carrots, quartered lengthwise

1 medium onion, halved, thinly sliced

1 lb chicken breast strips for stir-frying

2 cups frozen cut green beans, thawed

1 can (14.5 oz) diced tomatoes, undrained

1 jar (4.5 oz) sliced mushrooms, drained

1 jar (12 oz) brown mushroom gravy

¼ cup all-purpose flour

¼ teaspoon salt

1 can (8 oz) Pillsbury refrigerated crescent dinner rolls (8 rolls)

1 tablespoon sesame seed

Cooking spray

1 Heat oven to 375°F. Spray 13x9-inch (3-quart) glass baking dish or 3-quart oval casserole with cooking spray. In 10-inch skillet, heat oil over medium-high heat until hot. Add carrots and onion; cook and stir 3 minutes. Add chicken; cook 4 to 5 minutes, stirring frequently, until chicken is no longer pink in center and vegetables are tender.

2 Add green beans, tomatoes and mushrooms; mix well. In small bowl, mix gravy, flour and salt; blend well. Add to chicken mixture; cook and stir until mixture is bubbly. Remove from heat. Pour into baking dish.

3 Separate dough into 8 triangles. Starting from shortest side of each triangle, roll up halfway; arrange over hot chicken mixture so pointed ends are toward center. Spray rolls with cooking spray; sprinkle with sesame seed.

4 Bake 18 to 23 minutes or until crescent rolls are deep golden brown.

1 Serving: Calories 270; Total Fat 11g (Saturated Fat 2g, Trans Fat nc); Cholesterol 35mg; Sodium 720mg; Total Carbohydrate 25g (Dietary Fiber 3g); Protein 17g **Exchanges:** 1½ Starch, 1½ Other Carbohydrate, 1 Vegetable, 1½ Very Lean Meat, 1½ Fat

grands! mini chicken pot pies

prep time: **20 Minutes** • start to finish: **45 Minutes** • **8 pot pies**

2 **cups frozen mixed vegetables, thawed**

1 **cup diced cooked chicken**

1 **can (10¾ oz) condensed cream of chicken soup**

1 **can (16.3 oz) Pillsbury Grands! Flaky Layers refrigerated biscuits (8 biscuits)**

1 Heat oven to 375°F. Grease 8 regular-size muffin cups with shortening or cooking spray. In medium bowl, mix vegetables, chicken and soup.

2 Separate dough into 8 biscuits. Press each biscuit into 5½-inch round. Place 1 round in each muffin cup. Firmly press in bottom and up side, forming ¾-inch rim. Spoon generous ⅓ cup chicken mixture into each. Pull edges of dough over filling toward center; pleat and pinch dough gently to hold in place.

3 Bake 20 to 22 minutes or until biscuits are golden brown. Cool 1 minute; remove from pan.

1 Pot Pie: Calories 270; Total Fat 12g (Saturated Fat 3g, Trans Fat 2g); Cholesterol 20mg; Sodium 830mg; Total Carbohydrate 33g (Dietary Fiber 1g); Protein 9g **Exchanges:** 2 Starch, ½ Very Lean Meat, 2 Fat **Carbohydrate Choices:** 2

Easy Success Tips

If your family loves cheese, sprinkle some shredded Cheddar cheese over each puff about 5 minutes before the end of the bake time.

Substitute 2 cups of any frozen (thawed) vegetables you have on hand, such as broccoli, corn, peas or green beans, for the mixed vegetables.

chicken–blue cheese crostata with spicy tart cherry sauce

prep time: 25 Minutes • **start to finish:** 1 Hour • 6 servings

4	slices bacon, chopped
2½	cups chopped cooked chicken
1½	cups chopped unpeeled apples
1½	cups crumbled blue cheese (6 oz)
1	Pillsbury refrigerated pie crust, softened as directed on box
¼	teaspoon pepper
½	cup red tart cherry preserves
2	teaspoons sambal oelek (chili paste)
1	tablespoon water

1 Heat oven to 425°F. Line 12-inch round pizza pan with cooking parchment paper.

2 In 12-inch nonstick skillet, cook bacon over medium-high heat 7 to 8 minutes, stirring occasionally, until crisp; drain on paper towels. In large bowl, mix bacon, chicken, apples and blue cheese.

3 Unroll pie crust on work surface; roll into 12-inch round. Place on pan. Spoon chicken mixture in center of crust to within 2 inches of edge. Fold edge of crust over filling, pleating crust as necessary. Sprinkle with pepper. Bake 25 to 30 minutes or until crust is deep golden brown and cheese is melted. Cool 5 minutes.

4 Meanwhile, in small microwavable bowl mix preserves, chili paste and water; microwave on High 30 to 40 seconds or until thoroughly heated. Drizzle each serving with about 2 tablespoons sauce.

1 Serving: Calories 460; Total Fat 23g (Saturated Fat 11g, Trans Fat 0g); Cholesterol 80mg; Sodium 800mg; Total Carbohydrate 40g (Dietary Fiber 1g); Protein 25g **Exchanges:** 2½ Starch, 1½ Very Lean Meat, 1 Medium-Fat Meat, 3 Fat **Carbohydrate Choices:** 2½

parmesan crescent-topped chicken à la king

prep time: 40 Minutes • **start to finish:** 1 Hour • 8 servings

Casserole

- 2 tablespoons butter
- 1½ lb boneless skinless chicken breasts, cut into bite-size pieces
- 1½ cups carrot strips (1½x¼x¼ inch)
- 1½ cups fresh or frozen cut green beans
- 1 cup thin red bell pepper strips (1 medium)
- ½ cup sliced green onions (8 medium)
- ½ cup all-purpose flour
- ½ teaspoon dried Italian seasoning
- ¼ teaspoon salt
- ⅛ teaspoon pepper
- 1 can (14½ oz) chicken broth
- ¾ cup milk
- ¼ cup grated Parmesan cheese

Topping

- 1 can (8 oz) Pillsbury refrigerated crescent dinner rolls (8 rolls)
- 1 egg white, beaten
- 2 tablespoons grated Parmesan cheese

1 Heat oven to 375°F. In 10- to 12-inch skillet, melt butter over medium-high heat. Add chicken; cook and stir 3 minutes. Add carrots, green beans, bell pepper and green onions; cover and cook, stirring occasionally, until chicken is no longer pink and vegetables are crisp-tender.

2 Add flour, Italian seasoning, salt and pepper to skillet. Stir in broth and milk. Heat to boiling, stirring constantly. Stir in ¼ cup Parmesan cheese. Spoon into ungreased 2½-quart oval casserole or 13x9-inch (3-quart) glass baking dish.

3 Separate dough into 8 triangles. Starting at short side of triangle, roll each triangle up halfway. Arrange over hot chicken mixture with tips toward center. DO NOT OVERLAP. Brush crescent rolls with egg white; sprinkle with 2 tablespoons Parmesan cheese. Cover edges of crescent dough with strips of foil.

4 Bake 18 to 22 minutes or until crescent rolls are golden brown.

1 Serving: Calories 310; Total Fat 13g (Saturated Fat 5g, Trans Fat 0g); Cholesterol 65mg; Sodium 630mg; Total Carbohydrate 23g (Dietary Fiber 2g); Protein 26g **Exchanges:** 1½ Starch, 3 Very Lean Meat, 2 Fat **Carbohydrate Choices:** 1½

easy caprese pizza bake

prep time: 20 Minutes • **start to finish:** 40 Minutes • 5 servings

3 teaspoons olive oil

1 lb bulk sweet Italian sausage

4 cups pizza sauce

¼ cup water

½ cup fresh basil leaves, chopped

1 can (12 oz) Pillsbury Grands! Jr. Golden Layers refrigerated buttermilk biscuits (10 biscuits)

20 fresh mozzarella ciliegine (cherry-size) cheese balls (from 8-oz container)

¼ cup shredded Parmesan cheese (1 oz)

1 Heat oven to 400°F. In 12-inch skillet, heat 1 teaspoon of the oil over medium heat. Add sausage; cook 4 to 5 minutes, stirring frequently, until browned. Stir in pizza sauce, water and ¼ cup of the basil; cook over medium-low heat 2 to 3 minutes or until thoroughly heated.

2 Meanwhile, separate dough into 10 biscuits; separate each biscuit into 2 layers to create 20 biscuits. Place 1 cheese ball in center of each biscuit. Carefully stretch dough around cheese; pinch edges to seal completely.

3 Pour meat sauce into ungreased 13x9-inch (3-quart) glass baking dish. Place biscuits seam side down on top of sauce. Brush tops of biscuits with remaining 2 teaspoons oil. Bake 13 to 20 minutes or until biscuits are golden brown and sauce is bubbly. Sprinkle with shredded cheese and remaining ¼ cup basil.

1 Serving: Calories 700; Total Fat 42g (Saturated Fat 17g, Trans Fat 0g); Cholesterol 75mg; Sodium 2140mg; Total Carbohydrate 50g (Dietary Fiber 4g); Protein 31g **Exchanges:** 2½ Starch, ½ Other Carbohydrate, 1 Vegetable, 1 Medium-Fat Meat, 2 High-Fat Meat, 4 Fat **Carbohydrate Choices:** 3

moroccan chicken crescent casserole

prep time: 25 Minutes • start to finish: 50 Minutes • 6 servings

1 tablespoon olive oil

6 boneless skinless chicken breasts (about 1½ lb), cut into bite-size pieces

½ cup chopped onion

½ cup sliced carrot

1 can (14.5 oz) diced fire-roasted or regular tomatoes, undrained

1 tablespoon tomato paste

3 tablespoons chopped fresh parsley

3 tablespoons chopped fresh cilantro

1½ teaspoons paprika

½ teaspoon salt

½ teaspoon ground cumin

¼ to ½ teaspoon ground cinnamon

⅛ teaspoon ground red pepper (cayenne)

1 can (8 oz) Pillsbury refrigerated crescent dinner rolls (8 rolls)

1 egg, beaten

1 tablespoon sliced almonds

1 Heat oven to 375°F. In 12-inch skillet, heat oil over medium-high heat. Add chicken, onion and carrot; cook and stir about 7 minutes or until chicken is browned and no longer pink in center. Stir in tomatoes, tomato paste, parsley, cilantro, paprika, salt, cumin, cinnamon and red pepper. Cook and stir about 5 minutes or until thoroughly heated.

2 Into ungreased 11x7-inch (2-quart) glass baking dish or 9½- or 10-inch deep-dish pie plate, pour hot chicken mixture. Immediately unroll dough over chicken mixture; pinch edges and perforations to seal. Brush dough with beaten egg; sprinkle with almonds.

3 Bake 18 to 25 minutes or until deep golden brown. If desired, garnish with additional fresh cilantro.

1 Serving: Calories 320; Total Fat 13g (Saturated Fat 4g, Trans Fat 0g); Cholesterol 70mg; Sodium 690mg; Total Carbohydrate 23g (Dietary Fiber 2g); Protein 29g **Exchanges:** 1 Starch, 1 Vegetable, 3½ Lean Meat, ½ Fat **Carbohydrate Choices:** 1½

Easy Success Tips

Add ¼ cup chopped, toasted, blanched almonds or raisins to the chicken mixture for added flavor and texture.

Be quick putting the casserole in the oven so that the dough gets completely cooked on the bottom.

chicken teriyaki galette

prep time: 20 Minutes • start to finish: 50 Minutes • 4 servings

1 tablespoon vegetable oil

1 medium yellow onion, thinly sliced

1 yellow, orange or red bell pepper, seeded and thinly sliced

1 cup shredded deli rotisserie chicken

¼ cup teriyaki sauce

1 Pillsbury refrigerated pie crust, softened as directed on box

⅓ cup shredded pepper Jack cheese

1 Heat oven to 375°F. In 10-inch skillet, heat oil over medium-high heat. Cook onion in oil 6 to 7 minutes, stirring frequently, until softened and beginning to caramelize slightly. Add bell pepper; cook 4 to 5 minutes longer or until tender. Add chicken and teriyaki sauce to skillet. Cook about 2 minutes longer or until sauce evaporates slightly and chicken is warmed through.

2 Unroll pie crust on ungreased cookie sheet. Place onion mixture on crust, leaving 1½-inch border around edge. Fold edge of crust over filling, pleating crust as necessary. Sprinkle top with cheese.

3 Bake 20 to 25 minutes or until crust is dark golden brown and cheese is melted. Cool 5 minutes before serving.

1 Serving: Calories 380; Total Fat 21g (Saturated Fat 8g, Trans Fat 0g); Cholesterol 45mg; Sodium 1180mg; Total Carbohydrate 31g (Dietary Fiber 1g); Protein 15g **Exchanges:** ½ Starch, 1½ Other Carbohydrate, 1 Lean Meat, 1 High-Fat Meat, 2 Fat **Carbohydrate Choices:** 2

Easy Success Tip

Serve the galette with a crisp mixed-greens salad topped with your favorite dressing.

mediterranean chicken-vegetable galette

prep time: 15 Minutes • **start to finish: 55 Minutes** • **8 servings**

1 bag (11.8 oz) frozen Mediterranean blend vegetables

1 cup ricotta cheese

¼ cup grated Parmesan cheese

1 to 1½ teaspoons grated lemon peel

1 teaspoon salt

¼ teaspoon pepper

1 Pillsbury refrigerated pie crust, softened as directed on box

2 cups cooked roasted chicken breast strips (9 oz)

1 egg, beaten

1 Heat oven to 375°F. Spray large cookie sheet with cooking spray. Microwave frozen vegetables as directed on bag.

2 Meanwhile, in small bowl, mix ricotta cheese, 3 tablespoons of the Parmesan cheese, ½ to 1 teaspoon of the lemon peel, ½ teaspoon of the salt and ⅛ teaspoon of the pepper.

3 Unroll pie crust on cookie sheet. Spread cheese mixture over crust to within 1¼ inches of edge.

4 In large bowl, mix chicken strips and remaining ½ teaspoon lemon peel, ½ teaspoon salt and ⅛ teaspoon pepper. Add cooked vegetables; mix well. Spoon over cheese.

5 Fold edge of crust over filling, pleating crust as necessary. Brush crust edge with egg. Sprinkle crust edge and filling with remaining 1 tablespoon Parmesan cheese.

6 Bake 25 to 35 minutes or until crust is golden brown. Let stand 5 minutes.

1 Serving: Calories 260; Total Fat 13g (Saturated Fat 5g, Trans Fat 0g); Cholesterol 65mg; Sodium 670mg; Total Carbohydrate 19g (Dietary Fiber 0g); Protein 16g **Exchanges:** ½ Starch, ½ Other Carbohydrate, ½ Vegetable, 1 Very Lean Meat, 1 Medium-Fat Meat, 1½ Fat **Carbohydrate Choices:** 1

southwestern chicken pot pie

prep time: 10 Minutes • start to finish: 50 Minutes • 5 servings

2 cups chopped cooked chicken

¾ cup chopped red bell pepper

¾ cup frozen whole kernel corn, thawed

½ teaspoon ground cumin

1 can (15 oz) black beans, drained, rinsed

1 jar (12 oz) chicken gravy

1 can (10.2 oz) Pillsbury Grands! Flaky Layers refrigerated biscuits (5 biscuits)

¼ teaspoon chili powder

¾ cup shredded Cheddar cheese (3 oz)

2 tablespoons coarsely chopped fresh cilantro

1 Heat oven to 400°F. Grease 8-inch square (2-quart) glass baking dish.

2 In large bowl, mix chicken, bell pepper, corn, cumin, beans and gravy. Spoon into baking dish.

3 Bake 20 minutes. Remove baking dish from oven. Reduce oven temperature to 350°F. Separate dough into 5 biscuits. Arrange biscuits over chicken mixture; sprinkle biscuits with chili powder. Sprinkle cheese over chicken mixture around biscuits.

4 Bake at 350°F 15 to 18 minutes or until biscuits are golden brown and mixture is hot. Garnish with cilantro.

1 Serving: Calories 520; Total Fat 23g (Saturated Fat 8g, Trans Fat 2.5g); Cholesterol 70mg; Sodium 1300mg; Total Carbohydrate 48g (Dietary Fiber 6g); Protein 31g **Exchanges:** 3 Starch, 3 Other Carbohydrate, 3 Lean Meat, 2½ Fat **Carbohydrate Choices:** 2½

Easy Success Tips

To save time, the chicken mixture can be simmered on the stovetop instead of baked in the oven. Place chicken and gravy mixture in large saucepan. Heat to boiling and cook until hot, about 5 minutes. Immediately spoon hot chicken and gravy into baking dish; top with biscuits, and continue as directed for baking the biscuits.

It's easy to dress up servings of this pot pie with salsa, sour cream and a sprinkling of red and green jalapeño pepper slices.

home-style turkey and biscuit casserole

prep time: 15 Minutes • **start to finish:** 50 Minutes • 4 servings

1 can (10¾ oz) condensed cream of celery soup

½ cup milk

2 cups frozen mixed vegetables

2 cups cubed cooked turkey

1 cup chive-and-onion sour cream

¼ teaspoon poultry seasoning

4 Pillsbury™ Grands!™ frozen buttermilk biscuits (from 25-oz bag)

1 Heat oven to 375°F. Spray 8-inch square (2-quart) glass baking dish with cooking spray. In 2-quart saucepan, mix soup, milk and vegetables. Heat to boiling over medium heat, stirring occasionally to prevent sticking.

2 Stir in turkey, sour cream and poultry seasoning. Cook and stir just until thoroughly heated. Spoon into baking dish. Arrange frozen biscuits over hot mixture.

3 Bake uncovered 30 to 35 minutes or until biscuits are golden brown.

1 Serving: Calories 560; Total Fat 30g (Saturated Fat 12g, Trans Fat 4.5g); Cholesterol 105mg; Sodium 1240mg; Total Carbohydrate 42g (Dietary Fiber 5g); Protein 30g **Exchanges:** 2 Starch, 1 Other Carbohydrate, 3½ Lean Meat, 3½ Fat **Carbohydrate Choices:** 3

Easy Success Tip

If you're concerned about sodium, use home-cooked leftover turkey to make this hearty casserole. Some brands of packaged cubed turkey contain high salt levels.

cheeseburger crescent casserole

prep time: 10 Minutes • **start to finish:** 30 Minutes • 8 servings

1   lb lean (at least 80%) ground beef
½   cup ketchup
¼   cup dill pickle relish
1½ cups shredded American cheese (6 oz)
1   can (8 oz) Pillsbury refrigerated crescent dinner rolls (8 rolls)

1 Heat oven to 375°F. In 10-inch skillet, cook beef over medium heat 8 to 10 minutes, stirring occasionally, until brown and thoroughly cooked; drain. Stir in ketchup, relish and 1 cup of the cheese. Spoon into ungreased 9- or 10-inch glass pie plate.

2 Separate dough into 8 triangles; roll up 1 inch on shortest side of each dough triangle. Place dough on top of meat mixture with tips toward center. Sprinkle with remaining ½ cup cheese.

3 Bake 15 to 20 minutes or until cheese is melted.

1 Serving: Calories 360; Total Fat 22g (Saturated Fat 10g, Trans Fat 2.5g); Cholesterol 75mg; Sodium 620mg; Total Carbohydrate 18g (Dietary Fiber 0g); Protein 22g **Exchanges:** ½ Starch, ½ Other Carbohydrate, 3 Medium-Fat Meat, 1½ Fat **Carbohydrate Choices:** 1

spicy unstuffed peppers casserole

prep time: **25 Minutes** • start to finish: **45 Minutes** • **10 servings**

1 box (6.2 oz) fast-cooking long-grain and wild rice mix (with seasoning packet)

1½ lb lean (at least 80%) ground beef

1 tablespoon olive oil

2 large red, green or yellow bell peppers, cut into 1-inch pieces (about 4 cups)

3 cloves garlic, finely chopped

1 can (14.5 oz) diced tomatoes, undrained

2 chipotle chiles in adobo sauce (from 7-oz can), finely chopped

1 can (12 oz) Pillsbury Grands! Jr. Golden Layers refrigerated buttermilk biscuits (10 biscuits)

1 Heat oven to 375°F. Spray 13x9-inch (3-quart) glass baking dish with cooking spray.

2 Cook rice as directed on package. Meanwhile, in 12-inch nonstick skillet, cook beef over medium-high heat 5 to 7 minutes, stirring occasionally, until thoroughly cooked. Remove beef from skillet; drain well.

3 In same skillet, heat oil over medium heat. Cook bell peppers in oil 7 minutes, stirring occasionally, until crisp-tender. Add garlic; cook and stir 1 minute. Stir in tomatoes, chiles and beef. Heat to boiling; remove from heat.

4 Separate dough into 10 biscuits. Spread rice evenly in bottom of baking dish. Spoon hot beef mixture over rice. Top with biscuits. Bake immediately to ensure that bottoms of biscuits bake completely.

5 Bake uncovered 18 to 20 minutes or until thoroughly heated and biscuits are golden.

1 Serving: Calories 310; Total Fat 13g (Saturated Fat 4g, Trans Fat 1.5g); Cholesterol 40mg; Sodium 760mg; Total Carbohydrate 32g (Dietary Fiber 1g); Protein 16g **Exchanges:** 2 Starch, ½ Vegetable, ½ Lean Meat, 1 Medium-Fat Meat, 1 Fat **Carbohydrate Choices:** 2

Easy Success Tip

Easily adjust the heat in this dish by varying the amount of chipotle chiles used.

two-bean burger casserole

prep time: **25 Minutes** • start to finish: **45 Minutes** • **6 servings**

6 slices bacon

1 lb lean (at least 80%) ground beef

1 cup chopped onions (2 medium)

1 can (16 oz) baked beans with bacon and brown sugar sauce, undrained

1 can (15 oz) dark red kidney beans, drained, ¼ cup liquid reserved

¼ cup packed brown sugar

¼ cup ketchup

3 tablespoons white vinegar

1 can Pillsbury refrigerated original breadsticks

1 tablespoon milk

2 teaspoons sesame seed

1 Heat oven to 400°F. In 12-inch nonstick skillet, cook bacon over medium heat, turning once, until crisp. Drain on paper towels; crumble bacon. Drain drippings from skillet.

2 In same skillet, cook beef and onions over medium-high heat, stirring occasionally, until beef is thoroughly cooked; drain. Stir in bacon, baked beans, kidney beans with reserved ¼ cup liquid, brown sugar, ketchup and vinegar. Reduce heat to medium-low; cook until bubbly, stirring occasionally. Pour into ungreased 11x7-inch (2-quart) glass baking dish.

3 Unroll dough; separate into 12 breadsticks. Arrange in lattice design over bean mixture, overlapping as necessary to fit. Brush dough with milk; sprinkle with sesame seed.

4 Bake 15 to 20 minutes or until breadsticks are golden brown and filling is bubbly.

1 Serving: Calories 590; Total Fat 19g (Saturated Fat 7g, Trans Fat 0.5g); Cholesterol 65mg; Sodium 1040mg; Total Carbohydrate 74g (Dietary Fiber 7g); Protein 31g **Exchanges:** 3 Starch, 2 Other Carbohydrate, 3 Medium-Fat Meat **Carbohydrate Choices:** 5

Easy Success Tips

Brushing milk on the breadstick dough helps the breadsticks brown more evenly. For soft, moist breadsticks, brush dough with melted butter before sprinkling with sesame seed and baking. If you want a shiny, glossy crust, brush beaten egg over dough before baking.

If you don't own a 12-inch skillet, use an electric skillet or a Dutch oven.

cheeseburger pot pie

prep time: 20 Minutes • start to finish: 40 Minutes • 6 servings

1½ lb lean (at least 80%) ground beef

1 small onion, chopped (⅓ cup)

¾ cup ketchup

2 tablespoons chopped dill pickle, if desired

⅛ teaspoon pepper

1 cup shredded sharp Cheddar cheese (4 oz)

1 Pillsbury refrigerated pie crust, softened as directed on box

1 Heat oven to 450°F. In 10-inch skillet, cook beef and onion over medium-high heat 5 to 7 minutes, stirring occasionally, until beef is thoroughly cooked; drain. Reduce heat to medium. Stir in ketchup, pickle and pepper; cook 2 to 3 minutes or until thoroughly heated.

2 In ungreased 9-inch glass pie plate, spread beef mixture. Sprinkle with cheese. Unroll pie crust over beef mixture; seal edge and flute. Cut slits in several places in top crust.

3 Bake 13 to 20 minutes or until crust is golden brown and filling is bubbly. During last 10 minutes of baking, cover crust edge with strips of foil to prevent excessive browning.

1 Serving: Calories 460; Total Fat 28g (Saturated Fat 12g, Trans Fat 1g); Cholesterol 95mg; Sodium 650mg; Total Carbohydrate 26g (Dietary Fiber 0g); Protein 25g **Exchanges:** 1½ Starch, 3 Medium-Fat Meat, 2½ Fat **Carbohydrate Choices:** 2

Easy Success Tips

For milder flavor, you can use an American-Cheddar cheese blend instead of the sharp Cheddar.

It's easy to substitute ground turkey for the beef if you prefer it.

country beef pot pie

prep time: 35 Minutes • start to finish: 1 Hour 20 Minutes • 6 servings

1 box Pillsbury refrigerated pie crusts, softened as directed on box

1 tablespoon vegetable oil

¾ lb boneless beef sirloin steak, cut into ½-inch cubes

1 medium onion, chopped (½ cup)

1 jar (12 oz) beef gravy

1 tablespoon cornstarch

2 teaspoons sugar

⅛ teaspoon pepper

2 cups frozen mixed vegetables

2 cups frozen southern-style hash-brown potatoes (from 32-oz bag)

Sesame seed, if desired

1 Heat oven to 400°F. Make pie crusts as directed on box for Two-Crust Pie using 9-inch glass pie plate.

2 In 10-inch skillet, heat oil over medium-high heat until hot. Add beef and onion; cook and stir until beef is browned. Drain.

3 In small bowl, mix gravy, cornstarch, sugar and pepper. Add to beef in skillet. Stir in vegetables and potatoes. Cook about 5 minutes, stirring occasionally, until vegetables are thawed.

4 Spoon mixture into crust-lined pie plate. Top with second crust; seal edges and flute. Cut slits in several places in top crust; sprinkle with sesame seed.

5 Bake 35 to 45 minutes or until golden brown. Let stand 10 minutes before serving.

1 Serving: Calories 570; Total Fat 30g (Saturated Fat 11g, Trans Fat 1.5g); Cholesterol 30mg; Sodium 910mg; Total Carbohydrate 57g (Dietary Fiber 6g); Protein 19g **Exchanges:** 3½ Starch, 1½ Vegetable, ½ Lean Meat, 5 Fat **Carbohydrate Choices:** 4

spicy mexican casserole

prep time: 15 Minutes • start to finish: 50 Minutes • 6 servings

1 lb chorizo or pork sausage

1 can (11 oz) whole kernel corn with red and green peppers, drained

5 eggs

¼ teaspoon salt

⅛ teaspoon pepper

¼ cup chopped green onions (4 medium)

2 tablespoons chopped fresh cilantro

1½ cups shredded Cheddar-Jack with jalapeño peppers cheese blend (6 oz)

1 can (8 oz) Pillsbury Crescent Recipe Creations refrigerated seamless dough sheet

Sour cream, if desired

Chunky-style salsa, if desired

1 Heat oven to 375°F. In 10-inch skillet, cook sausage over medium-high heat, stirring frequently, until thoroughly cooked; drain. Stir in corn. Spoon into ungreased 11x7-inch (2-quart) glass baking dish.

2 In medium bowl, beat eggs, salt and pepper. Stir in green onions and cilantro. Pour evenly over sausage mixture. Sprinkle with cheese.

3 Unroll dough; place on top of cheese.

4 Bake 23 to 28 minutes or until golden brown. Cool 5 minutes. Cut into 6 rows by 2 rows. Top with sour cream and salsa.

1 Serving: Calories 600; Total Fat 42g (Saturated Fat 18g, Trans Fat 0g); Cholesterol 255mg; Sodium 1490mg; Total Carbohydrate 28g (Dietary Fiber 1g); Protein 29g **Exchanges:** 1½ Starch, ½ Other Carbohydrate, 3½ High-Fat Meat, 2½ Fat **Carbohydrate Choices:** 2

Easy Success Tip

If your family doesn't like the taste of cilantro, simply leave it out.

crescent-topped ratatouille casserole

prep time: 25 Minutes • start to finish: 1 Hour 10 Minutes • 6 servings

1 tablespoon olive or vegetable oil

1 small eggplant (1¼ lb), cut into ¾-inch cubes (4 cups)

1 medium zucchini, sliced

1 medium onion, sliced

1 medium green bell pepper, cut into 1-inch pieces

1 clove garlic, finely chopped

1 can (14.5 oz) diced tomatoes, undrained

1 can (8 oz) tomato sauce

½ teaspoon dried basil leaves

¼ teaspoon Italian seasoning

⅛ teaspoon coarse ground black pepper

1 can (15.5 oz) dark red kidney beans, drained, rinsed

1 can (8 oz) Pillsbury refrigerated crescent dinner rolls (8 rolls)

2 tablespoons grated Parmesan cheese

1 tablespoon chopped fresh parsley, if desired

1 In 10-inch skillet, heat oil over medium-high heat until hot. Add eggplant, zucchini, onion, bell pepper and garlic; cook and stir 4 to 6 minutes or until vegetables are lightly browned.

2 Reduce heat to medium-low. Stir in tomatoes, tomato sauce, basil, Italian seasoning and black pepper. Cover; simmer about 10 minutes or until vegetables are crisp-tender. Stir in beans; cook 5 minutes longer.

3 Meanwhile, remove dough from can in 2 rolled sections; do not unroll dough. Cut each roll into 4 slices; cut each slice into quarters. Place cheese in 1-quart resealable food-storage plastic bag; add crescent pieces, seal bag and shake to coat.

4 Heat oven to 375°F. Spray 11x7-inch (2-quart) glass baking dish with cooking spray. Spoon eggplant mixture into baking dish. Arrange crescent pieces on top.

5 Bake 17 to 20 minutes or until crescents are golden brown. Sprinkle with parsley.

1 Serving: Calories 320; Total Fat 12g (Saturated Fat 3.5g, Trans Fat 2g); Cholesterol 0mg; Sodium 620mg; Total Carbohydrate 43g (Dietary Fiber 8g); Protein 11g **Exchanges:** 1½ Starch, ½ Other Carbohydrate, 3 Vegetable, 2 Fat **Carbohydrate Choices:** 3

Easy Success Tip

The eggplant mixture can be made a day ahead of time and refrigerated, covered. To complete the casserole, heat the ratatouille in the oven or microwave until bubbly. Top with the biscuit pieces, and bake as directed.

veggie egg bake

prep time: 15 Minutes • **start to finish:** 1 Hour 20 Minutes • 8 servings

1 tablespoon olive oil

1 can (10.2 oz) Pillsbury Grands! Flaky Layers refrigerated original biscuits (5 biscuits)

1 box (9 oz) frozen chopped spinach, thawed, squeezed to drain

1 cup frozen whole kernel corn

½ cup chopped green onions (8 medium)

½ medium red bell pepper, chopped (½ cup)

2 cups shredded Cheddar-Jack cheese blend (8 oz)

6 eggs

1½ cups milk

1 teaspoon salt

½ to 1 teaspoon red pepper sauce

1 Heat oven to 325°F. Lightly brush the oil in bottom and up sides of 13x9-inch (3-quart) glass baking dish or soufflé dish. Separate dough into 5 biscuits. Cut each biscuit into 8 pieces; arrange evenly in dish. Layer spinach, corn, green onions, bell pepper and 1 cup of the cheese over dough.

2 In large bowl, beat eggs, milk, salt and pepper sauce with whisk until blended. Pour evenly over mixture in dish.

3 Bake uncovered 40 minutes. Top with remaining 1 cup cheese; bake 10 to 15 minutes longer or until edges are deep golden brown and center is set. Let stand 10 minutes before serving.

1 Serving: Calories 350; Total Fat 21g (Saturated Fat 9g, Trans Fat 2.5g); Cholesterol 190mg; Sodium 890mg; Total Carbohydrate 23g (Dietary Fiber 1g); Protein 17g **Exchanges:** 1 Starch, ½ Other Carbohydrate, 2 Medium-Fat Meat, 2 Fat **Carbohydrate Choices:** 1½

Easy Success Tip

Serve this hearty egg dish with fresh fruit, such as sliced pineapple and raspberries.

bacon and egg biscuit bake

prep time: **15 Minutes** • start to finish: **55 Minutes** • **4 servings**

4 Pillsbury Grands! frozen buttermilk biscuits (from 25-oz bag)

4 eggs

1 cup milk

1 can (11 oz) whole kernel corn with red and green peppers, drained

4 slices bacon, crisply cooked, crumbled (¼ cup)

1 cup shredded Swiss cheese (4 oz)

1 Heat oven to 350°F. Spray 11x7-inch (2-quart) glass baking dish with cooking spray. Place biscuits on cutting board to thaw, about 10 minutes.

2 Meanwhile, in medium bowl, beat eggs and milk with whisk until blended. Stir in corn, bacon and cheese.

3 Cut each biscuit into 8 pieces; arrange evenly in baking dish. Pour egg mixture over biscuits. Press down with back of spoon, making sure all biscuit pieces are covered with egg mixture.

4 Bake 30 to 35 minutes or until edges are golden brown and knife inserted in center comes out clean. Let stand 5 minutes before cutting.

1 Serving: Calories 500; Total Fat 25g (Saturated Fat 9g, Trans Fat 4g); Cholesterol 240mg; Sodium 1240mg; Total Carbohydrate 47g (Dietary Fiber 2g); Protein 23g **Exchanges:** 2½ Starch, ½ Other Carbohydrate, 2½ High-Fat Meat, ½ Fat **Carbohydrate Choices:** 3

Easy Success Tip
Diced ham can be substituted for the bacon.

ham and cheese omelet bake

prep time: 15 Minutes • **start to finish:** 1 Hour 15 Minutes • **8 servings**

1 box (10 oz) frozen broccoli and cheese sauce

1 can (10.2 oz) Pillsbury Grands! Flaky Layers refrigerated original biscuits (5 biscuits)

10 eggs

1½ cups milk

1 teaspoon ground mustard

Salt and pepper, if desired

2 cups diced cooked ham

1 small onion, chopped (⅓ cup)

1 cup shredded Cheddar cheese (4 oz)

1 cup shredded Swiss cheese (4 oz)

1 jar (4.5 oz) sliced mushrooms, drained

1 Heat oven to 350°F. Spray bottom only of 13x9-inch (3-quart) glass baking dish with cooking spray. Cut small slit in center of broccoli and cheese sauce pouch. Microwave on High 3 to 4 minutes, rotating pouch a quarter turn halfway through cooking time. Set aside to cool slightly.

2 Meanwhile, separate dough into 5 biscuits. Cut each biscuit into 8 pieces; arrange evenly in baking dish.

3 In large bowl, beat eggs, milk, mustard, salt and pepper with whisk until well blended. Stir in ham, onion, cheeses, mushrooms and broccoli and cheese sauce. Pour mixture over biscuit pieces. Press down with back of spoon, making sure all biscuit pieces are covered with egg mixture.

4 Bake 40 to 50 minutes or until edges are deep golden brown and center is set. Let stand 10 minutes before serving.

1 Serving: Calories 450; Total Fat 28g (Saturated Fat 11g, Trans Fat 2.5g); Cholesterol 315mg; Sodium 1090mg; Total Carbohydrate 22g (Dietary Fiber 1g); Protein 30g **Exchanges:** 1½ Starch, 3½ Medium-Fat Meat, 1½ Fat **Carbohydrate Choices:** 1½

pepperoni quiche squares

prep time: 20 Minutes • **start to finish:** 1 Hour 10 Minutes • 12 servings

1 can (8 oz) Pillsbury Crescent Recipe Creations refrigerated seamless dough sheet

48 slices (1½-inch size) pepperoni

5 eggs

1 cup whipping cream

1½ teaspoons Italian seasoning

1 tablespoon olive oil

½ cup chopped green bell pepper

½ cup chopped onion (about 1 small)

1½ cups shredded mozzarella cheese (6 oz)

¾ cup pizza sauce or pasta sauce, heated, if desired

1 Heat oven to 300°F. Unroll dough sheet; press dough in bottom of ungreased 13x9-inch pan. Top with 24 slices of the pepperoni (6 rows by 4 rows).

2 In medium bowl, beat eggs, cream and Italian seasoning with whisk until well blended.

3 In 10-inch skillet, heat oil over medium heat. Add bell pepper and onion; cook 4 minutes, stirring occasionally, until crisp-tender. Stir vegetable mixture into egg mixture; pour over pepperoni in pan. Sprinkle with cheese. Layer with remaining 24 slices pepperoni.

4 Bake 35 to 45 minutes or until edges are light golden brown and center is set. Cool 5 minutes. Cut into 4 rows by 3 rows; place on plates. Drizzle 1 tablespoon pizza sauce over each serving.

1 Serving: Calories 270; Total Fat 20g (Saturated Fat 9g, Trans Fat 0g); Cholesterol 120mg; Sodium 600mg; Total Carbohydrate 11g (Dietary Fiber 0g); Protein 13g **Exchanges:** ½ Starch, 1½ High-Fat Meat, 1½ Fat **Carbohydrate Choices:** 1

lasagna pasta pies

prep time: 20 Minutes • **start to finish:** 1 Hour • 8 servings

1 cup uncooked rotini pasta (3 oz)

1 lb bulk Italian sausage

1½ cups tomato pasta sauce

¾ cup ricotta cheese

1 can (16.3 oz) Pillsbury Grands! refrigerated buttermilk biscuits (8 biscuits)

1 cup shredded mozzarella cheese (4 oz)

1 Heat oven to 350°F. Cook and drain pasta as directed on package. Meanwhile, in 10-inch skillet, cook sausage until no longer pink; drain. Stir in pasta sauce, ricotta cheese and cooked pasta; cook 1 minute.

2 Separate dough into 8 biscuits; press each biscuit to form 5½-inch round. Firmly press 1 biscuit in bottom and up side of each of 8 ungreased jumbo muffin cups, forming ¼-inch rim. Fill with sausage mixture; sprinkle with mozzarella cheese.

3 Bake 28 to 32 minutes or until golden brown. Cool 1 minute; remove from pan.

1 Serving: Calories 550; Total Fat 23g (Saturated Fat 11g, Trans Fat 0g); Cholesterol 40mg; Sodium 1420mg; Total Carbohydrate 62g (Dietary Fiber 2g); Protein 22g **Exchanges:** 3 Starch, 1 Other Carbohydrate, 2 Medium-Fat Meat, 2 Fat **Carbohydrate Choices:** 4

baked potato and bacon galette

prep time: 15 Minutes • start to finish: 50 Minutes • 4 servings

1 Pillsbury refrigerated pie crust, softened as directed on box

¼ cup sour cream

1 bag (19 oz) frozen roasted potatoes with garlic and herb sauce

½ cup shredded Cheddar cheese (2 oz)

2 tablespoons cooked real bacon bits

Chopped green onion, if desired

1 Heat oven to 375°F. Unroll pie crust on ungreased cookie sheet. Spread sour cream on center of crust, leaving 1½-inch border around edge.

2 Microwave potatoes as directed on bag. Transfer to medium bowl; toss with cheese. Spoon potato mixture on top of sour cream. Sprinkle with bacon. Fold edge of crust over filling, pleating crust as necessary.

3 Bake 25 to 30 minutes or until crust is golden brown. Let stand 5 minutes. Top with green onion.

1 Serving: Calories 400; Total Fat 22g (Saturated Fat 11g, Trans Fat 0g); Cholesterol 35mg; Sodium 930mg; Total Carbohydrate 41g (Dietary Fiber 1g); Protein 9g **Exchanges:** 2 Starch, ½ Other Carbohydrate, ½ High-Fat Meat, 3½ Fat **Carbohydrate Choices:** 3

Easy Success Tip

Cover and refrigerate any leftover galette and use it within 3 days. Reheat in the oven before serving.

roasted vegetable tart

prep time: 20 Minutes • **start to finish:** 1 Hour 45 Minutes • 8 servings

1 **Pillsbury refrigerated pie crust,** softened as directed on box

1 **small sweet potato,** peeled, cut into 1-inch cubes (2 cups)

1 **box (7 oz) frozen antioxidant blend of broccoli, carrots and sweet peppers,** thawed

½ **teaspoon salt**

¼ **teaspoon pepper**

1 **teaspoon dried thyme leaves**

4 **oz Brie cheese,** rind removed, sliced

¾ **cup whipping cream**

2 **eggs**

1 Heat oven to 425°F. Make pie crust as directed on box for One-Crust Baked Shell using 9-inch glass pie plate—except do not prick crust. Bake 8 to 10 minutes or until light golden brown. With back of wooden spoon, carefully press down crust.

2 Line 15x10x1-inch pan with foil; spray with cooking spray. Place sweet potato cubes in pan. Bake 15 minutes. Add vegetable blend. Sprinkle potatoes and vegetables with salt and pepper. Bake 15 to 20 minutes longer, stirring occasionally, until sweet potatoes and vegetables are tender. Reduce oven temperature to 350°F.

3 Spread roasted vegetables in bottom of baked pie crust. Sprinkle with thyme; top with cheese.

4 In medium bowl, beat cream and eggs with whisk until blended. Pour over vegetables and cheese. Bake at 350°F 25 to 30 minutes or until cheese is melted and knife inserted in center comes out clean. Let stand 10 minutes before serving.

1 Serving: Calories 270; Total Fat 20g (Saturated Fat 11g, Trans Fat 0g); Cholesterol 95mg; Sodium 420mg; Total Carbohydrate 16g (Dietary Fiber 0g); Protein 6g **Exchanges:** 1 Starch, ½ Medium-Fat Meat, 3½ Fat **Carbohydrate Choices:** 1

biscuit-topped vegetable casserole

prep time: **15 Minutes** • start to finish: **35 Minutes** • **10 servings**

2 tablespoons butter

1 cup chopped red bell pepper

½ cup chopped onion

1 jar (15 or 16 oz) Alfredo pasta sauce

¼ cup milk

1 bag (12 oz) frozen cut green beans, thawed

1 can (15.25 oz) whole kernel sweet corn, drained

½ to 1 teaspoon Sriracha sauce

1 can (7.5 oz) Pillsbury™ refrigerated buttermilk biscuits (10 biscuits)

2 tablespoons shredded Parmesan cheese

1 Heat oven to 375°F. Spray 8-inch square (2-quart) glass baking dish with cooking spray.

2 In 10-inch skillet, melt 1 tablespoon of the butter over medium-high heat. Cook bell pepper and onion in butter, stirring occasionally, about 5 minutes or until tender. Stir in Alfredo sauce, milk, beans, corn and Sriracha sauce. Increase heat to high; cook, stirring constantly, until mixture is thoroughly heated and bubbly. Spoon into baking dish.

3 Separate dough into 10 biscuits. Cut each biscuit in half crosswise. Arrange around edge of baking dish, overlapping slightly. In small microwavable bowl, microwave remaining 1 tablespoon butter on High about 20 seconds or until melted. Drizzle butter over biscuits, and sprinkle with cheese.

4 Bake 15 to 20 minutes or until biscuits are golden brown. Let stand 10 minutes before serving.

1 Serving: Calories 270; Total Fat 17g (Saturated Fat 10g, Trans Fat 0.5g); Cholesterol 50mg; Sodium 540mg; Total Carbohydrate 23g (Dietary Fiber 2g); Protein 7g **Exchanges:** 1 Starch, 1½ Vegetable, 3½ Fat **Carbohydrate Choices:** 1½

Easy Success Tip

Sriracha is a hot chili sauce that can be found in the Asian foods section of large supermarkets. Use less if you like your casserole milder or more for a spicier version.

rice and bean burrito pot pie

prep time: **20 Minutes** • start to finish: **1 Hour 10 Minutes** • **6 servings**

1 tablespoon olive or vegetable oil

1 large onion, chopped (1 cup)

2 cloves garlic, finely chopped

1 jalapeño chile, seeded, finely chopped

2 large tomatoes, chopped (2 cups)

2 cans (15 oz each) Spanish rice with bell peppers and onions

1 cup shredded Monterey Jack cheese (4 oz)

1 can (15 oz) pinto beans, drained, rinsed

1 can Pillsbury refrigerated original breadsticks

½ cup sour cream

1 Heat oven to 375°F. Spray 2-quart casserole or 11x7-inch (2-quart) glass baking dish with cooking spray.

2 In 10-inch skillet, heat oil over medium-high heat. Cook onion in oil about 5 minutes, stirring occasionally, until golden brown. Stir in garlic and chile; cook 1 minute, stirring constantly. Stir in tomatoes; cook until thoroughly heated. Remove from heat.

3 In medium bowl, mix rice and cheese; spread in bottom and ½ inch up side of casserole. Spread beans evenly over rice mixture. Top with tomato mixture.

4 Bake uncovered 20 minutes. Remove from oven. Unroll dough; separate into 12 breadsticks. Twist 10 breadsticks; carefully arrange crosswise in single layer over casserole. Stretch and twist remaining 2 breadsticks; place lengthwise across other strips of dough.

5 Bake 20 to 25 minutes longer or until breadsticks are golden brown. Let stand 5 minutes before serving. Serve with sour cream.

1 Serving: Calories 480; Total Fat 15g (Saturated Fat 8g, Trans Fat 0g); Cholesterol 30mg; Sodium 730mg; Total Carbohydrate 68g (Dietary Fiber 7g); Protein 17g **Exchanges:** 3 Starch, 1 Other Carbohydrate, 1 Vegetable, 1 Lean Meat, 2 Fat **Carbohydrate Choices:** 4½

Easy Success Tip

This pot pie is baked first without the breadsticks on top so the tomato mixture can get hot before adding the breadsticks.

balsamic roasted tomato–spinach-bacon pie

prep time: 35 Minutes • **start to finish: 1 Hour 20 Minutes** • **8 servings**

1 Pillsbury refrigerated pie crust, softened as directed on box

9 medium plum (Roma) tomatoes, halved lengthwise, seeded

2 cloves garlic, finely chopped

½ teaspoon Italian seasoning

⅛ teaspoon salt

⅛ teaspoon black pepper

2 tablespoons balsamic vinegar

2 tablespoons olive oil

3 eggs

4 oz (half of 8-oz container) mascarpone cheese, softened

1 box (9 oz) frozen chopped spinach, thawed, squeezed to drain

1 cup grated Parmesan cheese

2 or 3 dashes ground red pepper (cayenne), if desired

¼ teaspoon salt

½ teaspoon black pepper

6 slices bacon, crisply cooked, crumbled

1 Heat oven to 425°F. Place pie crust in 9-inch glass pie plate as directed on box for One-Crust Filled Pie; flute edge. Bake 6 to 8 minutes or until just beginning to brown. Remove from oven.

2 Line 15x10x1-inch pan with foil. Arrange tomatoes cut side up in single layer in pan. Sprinkle with garlic, Italian seasoning and ⅛ teaspoon each salt and black pepper. Drizzle with vinegar and oil. Roast 25 to 30 minutes or until tomatoes are very tender. Remove from oven. Reduce oven temperature to 375°F.

3 Meanwhile, in medium bowl, beat eggs with whisk. Add mascarpone cheese; beat until well blended. Stir in spinach, ½ cup of the Parmesan cheese, the red pepper, ¼ teaspoon salt and ½ teaspoon black pepper. Spread mixture evenly in partially baked crust.

4 Arrange roasted tomatoes, overlapping slightly, in single layer on spinach mixture. Sprinkle with remaining ½ cup Parmesan cheese and the bacon.

5 Bake at 375°F 25 to 35 minutes, covering edge of crust with strips of foil after 10 to 15 minutes, until filling is set in center and crust is golden brown. Let stand 10 minutes before serving.

1 Serving: Calories 300; Total Fat 20g (Saturated Fat 8g, Trans Fat 0g); Cholesterol 95mg; Sodium 630mg; Total Carbohydrate 17g (Dietary Fiber 1g); Protein 11g
Exchanges: 1 Starch, 1 Medium-Fat Meat, 3 Fat **Carbohydrate Choices:** 1

veggie lovers' pot pie

prep time: 30 Minutes • **start to finish:** 55 Minutes • 8 servings

3 tablespoons butter

1 large russet potato, peeled, cut into ½-inch pieces (about 2½ cups)

1 large onion, chopped (about 1 cup)

1 teaspoon dried thyme leaves

½ teaspoon salt

¼ teaspoon pepper

¼ cup all-purpose flour

1 can (14 oz) vegetable broth

1 bag (1 lb) frozen broccoli, cauliflower and carrots, thawed, well drained

¼ cup milk

3 tablespoons grated Parmesan cheese

1 can (8 oz) Pillsbury™ refrigerated garlic butter crescent dinner rolls (8 rolls)

1 Heat oven to 375°F. Spray 9- or 10-inch glass deep-dish pie plate with cooking spray. In 12-inch skillet, melt butter over medium-high heat. Add potato, onion, thyme, salt and pepper; cook and stir 10 to 12 minutes until potatoes are lightly browned.

2 Sprinkle flour over potato mixture. Cook and stir 1 minute. Stir in broth; heat to boiling. Reduce heat to low; cover and simmer about 8 minutes, stirring occasionally, until potatoes are almost tender. Remove from heat. Stir in thawed vegetables, milk and cheese. Spoon mixture into pie plate.

3 Separate dough into 8 triangles. Starting at short side of each triangle, roll up triangle halfway. Carefully arrange over vegetable mixture with tips toward center — do not overlap. Place pie plate on cookie sheet with sides.

4 Bake 20 to 25 minutes or until crust is golden brown.

1 Serving: Calories 230; Total Fat 12g (Saturated Fat 5g, Trans Fat 1.5g); Cholesterol 15mg; Sodium 690mg; Total Carbohydrate 25g (Dietary Fiber 3g); Protein 5g **Exchanges:** 1 Starch, ½ Other Carbohydrate, 1 Vegetable, 2 Fat **Carbohydrate Choices:** 1½

Easy Success Tips

Quickly and easily thaw the frozen vegetables by placing in a colander and running under warm water.

This pot pie is very versatile. Serve it as a meatless main dish or side dish!

deep-dish lasagna pie

prep time: 25 Minutes • **start to finish:** 1 Hour • **8 servings**

1 lb bulk Italian pork sausage

1 large onion, chopped (about 1 cup)

2 cups tomato pasta sauce

½ teaspoon dried oregano leaves

1 egg

1 container (15 oz) part-skim ricotta cheese

½ cup grated Parmesan cheese

2 cups shredded mozzarella cheese (8 oz)

2 cans Pillsbury refrigerated classic pizza crust

1 Heat oven to 425°F. Spray 13x9-inch (3-quart) glass baking dish with cooking spray. In 12-inch nonstick skillet, cook sausage and onion over medium-high heat 5 to 7 minutes, stirring occasionally, until sausage is no longer pink; drain well. Stir in pasta sauce and oregano; cook until thoroughly heated.

2 In medium bowl, beat egg with whisk. Stir in ricotta cheese, Parmesan cheese and 1½ cups of the mozzarella cheese.

3 Unroll dough for 1 pizza crust. Press in bottom and 1 inch up sides of dish. Spread cheese mixture over dough in bottom of dish. Spread sausage mixture over cheese mixture. Unroll dough for second pizza crust; place over sausage mixture, and press edges to seal. Cut 4 slits in top crust.

4 Bake uncovered 15 minutes. Cover dish with sheet of foil to prevent excessive browning. Bake 9 to 11 minutes longer or until crust is golden brown. Top with remaining ½ cup mozzarella cheese. Let stand 5 minutes before serving.

1 Serving: Calories 600; Total Fat 25g (Saturated Fat 11g, Trans Fat 0g); Cholesterol 85mg; Sodium 1530mg; Total Carbohydrate 64g (Dietary Fiber 3g); Protein 30g **Exchanges:** 2 Starch, 2½ Other Carbohydrate, 3 High-Fat Meat **Carbohydrate Choices:** 4

mexican bubble pizza

prep time: 15 Minutes • start to finish: 50 Minutes • 8 servings

1½ lb lean (at least 80%) ground beef

1 package (1 oz) taco seasoning mix

¾ cup water

1 can (10¾ oz) condensed tomato soup

1 can (16.3 oz) Pillsbury Grands! refrigerated buttermilk biscuits (8 biscuits)

2 cups shredded Cheddar cheese (8 oz)

2 cups shredded lettuce

2 medium tomatoes, chopped

1 cup chunky-style salsa

1 can (2¼ oz) sliced ripe olives, drained

1 container (8 oz) sour cream

3 green onions, sliced, if desired

1 Heat oven to 375°F. In 10-inch skillet, cook beef over medium-high heat 8 to 10 minutes or until thoroughly cooked, stirring frequently; drain. Add taco seasoning mix, water and soup; mix well. Heat to boiling. Reduce heat to low; simmer 3 minutes. Remove from heat.

2 Separate dough into 8 biscuits. Cut each biscuit into 8 pieces. Add pieces to beef mixture; stir gently. Spoon mixture into ungreased 13x9-inch pan.

3 Bake uncovered 18 to 23 minutes or until sauce is bubbly and biscuits are golden brown. Sprinkle with cheese. Bake 8 to 10 minutes longer or until cheese is bubbly.

4 To serve, cut pizza into 8 squares. Top each serving with remaining ingredients.

1 Serving: Calories 550; Total Fat 32g (Saturated Fat 15g, Trans Fat 3g); Cholesterol 95mg; Sodium 1660mg; Total Carbohydrate 38g (Dietary Fiber 1g); Protein 27g **Exchanges:** 1½ Starch, 1 Other Carbohydrate, 3½ Medium-Fat Meat, 3 Fat **Carbohydrate Choices:** 2½

Easy Success Tip

Instead of Cheddar cheese, try a Mexican cheese blend, or spice things up and use pepper-Jack cheese.

seafood crescent casserole

prep time: 20 Minutes • start to finish: 40 Minutes • 6 servings

2 teaspoons vegetable oil

⅓ cup sliced celery

3 tablespoons sliced green onions (3 medium)

1 clove garlic, finely chopped

1 cup frozen baby sweet peas

12 oz refrigerated flake-style imitation crabmeat

1 jar (4.5 oz) sliced mushrooms, drained

1¼ cups shredded Parmesan cheese (5 oz)

1 container (10 oz) refrigerated Alfredo pasta sauce

1 can (8 oz) Pillsbury refrigerated crescent dinner rolls (8 rolls)

1 Heat oven to 375°F. Spray 11x7-inch (2-quart) glass baking dish with cooking spray. In 10-inch skillet, heat oil over medium heat until hot. Add celery, green onions and garlic; cook 1 to 2 minutes, stirring occasionally, until vegetables begin to soften.

2 Stir in frozen peas, imitation crabmeat and mushrooms. Cook 3 to 5 minutes, stirring occasionally, until thoroughly heated. Reserve 2 tablespoons of the cheese for topping. Stir remaining cheese and the pasta sauce into crabmeat mixture; cook 3 to 5 minutes, stirring occasionally, until thoroughly heated and cheese is melted. Spoon into baking dish.

3 Unroll dough into 2 long rectangles; press perforations to seal. Place rectangles over crabmeat mixture; pinch center edges to seal. Press outside edges of dough to edges of baking dish. Cut several slits in dough to allow steam to escape. Sprinkle with reserved 2 tablespoons cheese.

4 Bake 15 to 20 minutes or until thoroughly heated and crust is golden brown. Cut into 6 squares.

1 Serving: Calories 480; Total Fat 30g (Saturated Fat 16g, Trans Fat 0.5g); Cholesterol 80mg; Sodium 1700mg; Total Carbohydrate 31g (Dietary Fiber 3g); Protein 26g **Exchanges:** 2 Starch, 2 Other Carbohydrate, 3 Medium-Fat Meat, 2 Fat **Carbohydrate Choices:** 2

Easy Success Tip

For a nutty cheese flavor, try Asiago in this casserole. Like Parmesan, Asiago is an Italian cheese aged for grating. Asiago that is less than a year old is a lovely table cheese.

Cherry Pie Cups (page 226)

dessert pies and pastries

apple slab pie

prep time: 20 Minutes • start to finish: 2 Hours 15 Minutes • 24 servings

1 box Pillsbury refrigerated pie crusts, softened as directed on box
1 cup granulated sugar
3 tablespoons all-purpose flour
1 teaspoon ground cinnamon
¼ teaspoon ground nutmeg
¼ teaspoon salt
4½ teaspoons lemon juice
9 cups thinly sliced peeled apples (9 medium)
1 cup powdered sugar
2 tablespoons milk

1 Heat oven to 450°F. Unroll pie crusts, and stack one on top of the other on lightly floured surface. Roll to 17x12-inch rectangle. Fit crust into ungreased 15x10x1-inch pan, pressing into corners. Fold extra pastry crust under, even with edges of pan; seal edges.

2 In large bowl, mix granulated sugar, flour, cinnamon, nutmeg, salt and lemon juice. Add apples; toss to coat. Spoon into crust-lined pan.

3 Bake 33 to 38 minutes or until crust is golden brown and filling is bubbly. Cool on cooling rack 45 minutes.

4 In small bowl, mix powdered sugar and milk until well blended. Drizzle over pie. Allow glaze to set before serving, about 30 minutes.

1 Serving: Calories 150; Total Fat 4g (Saturated Fat 1.5g, Trans Fat 0g); Cholesterol 0mg; Sodium 110mg; Total Carbohydrate 28g (Dietary Fiber 0g); Protein 0g **Exchanges:** 2 Other Carbohydrate, 1 Fat **Carbohydrate Choices:** 2

Easy Success Tip

Need to make dessert for a potluck or other large gathering? This is the perfect pie—it's easy to put together and serves a crowd.

caramel apple pie

prep time: 20 Minutes • start to finish: 2 Hours 5 Minutes • 8 servings

Crust

- 1 box Pillsbury refrigerated pie crusts, softened as directed on box
- ¼ cup finely chopped pecans

Filling

- ¾ cup sugar
- 2 tablespoons all-purpose flour
- 1 teaspoon ground cinnamon
- ⅛ teaspoon ground nutmeg
- 1 tablespoon lemon juice
- 6 cups sliced peeled apples (6 medium)

Topping

- ⅓ cup caramel topping
- ¼ cup chopped pecans

Serve with, If Desired

Vanilla ice cream

Caramel topping

1 Heat oven to 425°F. Make pie crusts as directed on box for Two-Crust Pie, using 9-inch glass pie plate. Sprinkle ¼ cup finely chopped pecans in bottom of crust-lined pie plate.

2 In large bowl, mix sugar, flour, cinnamon and nutmeg. Gently stir in lemon juice and apples. Spoon into crust-lined pie plate. Top with second crust; seal edge and flute. Cut slits or shapes in several places in top crust. If desired, brush crust with water; sprinkle lightly with sugar.

3 Bake 35 to 45 minutes or until apples are tender and crust is golden brown. After 15 to 20 minutes of bake time, cover edge of pie crust with foil to prevent excessive browning. Immediately after removing pie from oven, drizzle with ⅓ cup caramel topping; sprinkle with ¼ cup chopped pecans. Cool on cooling rack at least 1 hour before serving.

4 Serve warm pie with ice cream; drizzle with caramel topping.

1 Serving: Calories 440; Total Fat 19g (Saturated Fat 5g, Trans Fat 0g); Cholesterol 10mg; Sodium 270mg; Total Carbohydrate 67g (Dietary Fiber 2g); Protein 1g **Exchanges:** 1 Starch, 3½ Other Carbohydrate, 3½ Fat **Carbohydrate Choices:** 4½

Easy Success Tip

Chopped walnuts can be used instead of the pecans for a different nutty taste. If you have apple pie spice on hand, use 1¼ teaspoons instead of the cinnamon and nutmeg.

easy apple-raisin pie slices

prep time: 15 Minutes • **start to finish:** 1 Hour • 6 servings

1 Pillsbury refrigerated pie crust, softened as directed on box

¼ cup sugar

1 tablespoon all-purpose flour

½ teaspoon ground cinnamon

2 cups finely chopped, peeled baking apples

¼ cup raisins

1 tablespoon butter cut into pieces

1 tablespoon sugar

Ice cream, if desired

1 Heat oven to 425°F. Spray cookie sheet with cooking spray. Unroll crust in center of cookie sheet.

2 In medium bowl, mix ¼ cup sugar, the flour and cinnamon. Add apples and raisins; toss gently to coat. Spoon apple mixture lengthwise down center third of crust to form 5-inch-wide strip to within ½ inch of top and bottom ends, pressing lightly to distribute evenly. Dot apple mixture with butter.

3 Fold sides of crust to center, overlapping center slightly, to enclose apple mixture. Fold top and bottom ends over about ½ inch. Brush crust lightly with water; sprinkle with 1 tablespoon sugar.

4 Bake 20 to 25 minutes or until crust is golden brown. Cool 15 to 20 minutes. Cut crosswise into slices. Serve with ice cream.

1 Serving: Calories 260; Total Fat 11g (Saturated Fat 4.5g, Trans Fat 0g); Cholesterol 10mg; Sodium 160mg; Total Carbohydrate 39g (Dietary Fiber 0g); Protein 0g
Exchanges: ½ Starch, 2 Other Carbohydrate, 2 Fat **Carbohydrate Choices:** 2½

Easy Success Tip

To make ahead, bake the pie, but do not slice it. Cool, cover and refrigerate it for up to 1 day. Uncover, and reheat the pie at 350°F for 5 to 10 minutes or until warm.

caramel-apple-marshmallow tarts

prep time: 20 Minutes • start to finish: 1 Hour 10 Minutes • 8 tarts

1 box Pillsbury refrigerated pie crusts, softened as directed on box

1 cup apple pie filling with more fruit (from 21-oz can)

¾ cup miniature marshmallows

3 tablespoons caramel topping

1 Heat oven to 400°F. Unroll pie crusts on work surface. With 4½-inch round cutter, cut 4 rounds from each pie crust.

2 Spoon about 2 tablespoons pie filling onto center of each pie crust round. Firmly fold edge of crust over sides of filling, ruffling decoratively. Place on ungreased large cookie sheet.

3 Bake 15 to 20 minutes or until crust is golden brown. Sprinkle marshmallows over filling. Bake 3 to 4 minutes longer or until marshmallows are puffed and just beginning to brown. Cool completely, about 30 minutes.

4 Just before serving, drizzle about 1 teaspoon caramel topping over each tart.

1 Tart: Calories 220; Total Fat 9g (Saturated Fat 3g, Trans Fat 0g); Cholesterol 0mg; Sodium 170mg; Total Carbohydrate 34g (Dietary Fiber 0g); Protein 0g **Exchanges:** ½ Starch, 1½ Other Carbohydrate, 2 Fat **Carbohydrate Choices:** 2

Easy Success Tip

Make pie crust cookies with dough scraps. Reroll and cut the dough into shapes; sprinkle with cinnamon and sugar. Bake at 400°F for 7 to 9 minutes or until golden brown.

cinnamon-apple crostata

prep time: 20 Minutes • start to finish: 55 Minutes • 8 servings

1   Pillsbury refrigerated pie crust, softened as directed on box

½   cup sugar

4   teaspoons cornstarch

2   teaspoons ground cinnamon

4   cups thinly sliced peeled apples (4 medium)

1   teaspoon sugar

2   tablespoons chopped pecans or walnuts

Whipped cream or ice cream, if desired

1 Heat oven to 450°F. On ungreased cookie sheet, unroll pie crust.

2 In medium bowl, mix ½ cup sugar, the cornstarch and cinnamon. Gently stir in apples until evenly coated. Spoon filling mixture onto center of crust, spreading to within 2 inches of edge. Carefully fold 2-inch edge of crust over filling, pleating crust slightly as necessary. Brush crust edge with water; sprinkle with 1 teaspoon sugar.

3 Bake about 15 minutes or until crust is golden brown. Sprinkle pecans over filling. Bake 5 to 15 minutes longer or until apples are tender. Cool on cooling rack 15 minutes. Cut into wedges. Serve warm with whipped cream.

1 Serving: Calories 220; Total Fat 8g (Saturated Fat 2.5g, Trans Fat 0g); Cholesterol 0mg; Sodium 110mg; Total Carbohydrate 35g (Dietary Fiber 1g); Protein 0g **Exchanges:** 2½ Other Carbohydrate, 1½ Fat **Carbohydrate Choices:** 2

cranberry-apple napoleons

prep time: 30 Minutes • start to finish: 30 Minutes • 4 servings

Crust

- 1 Pillsbury refrigerated pie crust, softened as directed on box
- 1 tablespoon butter or margarine, melted
- 2 teaspoons granulated sugar

Filling

- 2 tablespoons butter
- 2 large apples, peeled, sliced
- ¼ cup sweetened dried cranberries
- ¼ cup packed brown sugar
- ½ teaspoon ground cinnamon

Topping

- 1 cup vanilla ice cream
- 2 tablespoons caramel topping
- 2 tablespoons chopped pecans, toasted*

1 Heat oven to 425°F. Unroll pie crust on work surface; brush with 1 tablespoon melted butter. Sprinkle with granulated sugar; cut into 8 wedges. Place on ungreased large cookie sheet. Bake 8 to 10 minutes or until golden brown.

2 Meanwhile, in 10-inch skillet, melt 2 tablespoons butter over medium-high heat. Add remaining filling ingredients; cook 3 to 4 minutes, stirring frequently, until apples are tender and mixture is slightly thickened.

3 Place 1 pie crust wedge on each of 4 dessert plates. Spoon about ½ cup filling onto each wedge; top with a second pie crust wedge. Top each with ¼ cup ice cream. Drizzle with caramel topping; sprinkle with pecans.

*To toast pecans, heat oven to 350°F. Spread pecans in ungreased shallow pan. Bake uncovered 8 to 10 minutes, stirring occasionally, until golden brown.

1 Serving: Calories 560; Total Fat 27g (Saturated Fat 13g, Trans Fat 0g); Cholesterol 45mg; Sodium 390mg; Total Carbohydrate 75g (Dietary Fiber 2g); Protein 3g **Exchanges:** 1 Starch, 1 Fruit, 3 Other Carbohydrate, 5½ Fat **Carbohydrate Choices:** 5

Easy Success Tip

To peel apples, use a swivel-bladed vegetable peeler. It peels more quickly than a knife and will remove the peel without taking much of the apple flesh.

gluten-free cherry hand pies

prep time: 20 Minutes • **start to finish:** 1 Hour • 8 pies

1 container Pillsbury Gluten Free refrigerated pie and pastry dough

1 cup gluten-free cherry pie filling (from 21-oz can)

½ cup powdered sugar

1½ to 2 teaspoons water

1 Heat oven to 425°F. Divide dough in half. Knead each half until softened and no longer crumbly. Flatten each into a round.

2 Place 1 round between 2 sheets of cooking parchment or waxed paper. Roll into 11½-inch round. Carefully peel off top sheet of paper. Replace paper to cover loosely. Carefully turn dough over and remove second sheet of paper. With 4-inch round cutter, cut out 5 rounds; place on 1 large or 2 small cooking parchment paper–lined cookie sheets.

3 Gather dough scraps; knead until ball forms. Flatten dough into a round. Using parchment as directed above, reroll dough scraps about ⅛ inch thick; cut out 2 additional rounds. Repeat to cut out 1 more round. Spoon 2 tablespoons pie filling onto center of each of 4 dough rounds. Top each with another round. Press edges with fork to seal. Cut slits in tops.

4 Repeat step 2 with remaining dough and filling.

5 Bake 12 to 14 minutes or until golden brown. Cool 5 minutes. In small bowl, mix powdered sugar and water until thin enough to drizzle; drizzle over warm pies. Serve warm or cool.

1 Pie: Calories 560; Total Fat 34g (Saturated Fat 12g, Trans Fat 0g); Cholesterol 0mg; Sodium 680mg; Total Carbohydrate 62g (Dietary Fiber 1g); Protein 1g **Exchanges:** ½ Starch, 3½ Other Carbohydrate, 6½ Fat **Carbohydrate Choices:** 4

Easy Success Tip

If you are cooking gluten free, always read labels to make sure each recipe ingredient is gluten free. Products and ingredient sources can change.

cherry pie cups

prep time: **15 Minutes** • start to finish: **35 Minutes** • **12 pie cups**

1 **box Pillsbury refrigerated pie crusts, softened as directed on box**

1 **can (21 oz) cherry pie filling**

1 Heat oven to 425°F. Unroll pie crusts on work surface. With 3½- or 4-inch round cutter, cut 6 rounds from each crust; discard scraps. Fit rounds into 12 ungreased regular-size muffin cups, pressing in gently. Spoon about 2 tablespoons pie filling into each crust-lined cup.

2 Bake 14 to 18 minutes or until edges are golden brown and filling is bubbly.

1 Pie Cup: Calories 170; Total Fat 7g (Saturated Fat 2.5g, Trans Fat 0g); Cholesterol 0mg; Sodium 110mg; Total Carbohydrate 26g (Dietary Fiber 0g); Protein 0g **Exchanges:** ½ Starch, 1 Other Carbohydrate, 1½ Fat **Carbohydrate Choices:** 2

Easy Success Tip

We love these little cherry pies but you could choose to change the flavor by simply using another flavor of pie filling. Why not try blueberry, peach or apple?

orange-cardamom-blueberry crostata

prep time: 10 Minutes • **start to finish: 1 Hour 5 Minutes** • **6 servings**

1 Pillsbury refrigerated pie crust, softened as directed on box

½ cup orange marmalade

2 tablespoons all-purpose flour

¼ teaspoon ground cardamom

2 cups fresh blueberries

1 egg yolk

2 teaspoons water

1 to 2 tablespoons coarse sugar

1 Heat oven to 425°F. Line 15x10x1-inch pan with cooking parchment paper.

2 Unroll pie crust in pan. In medium bowl, mix marmalade, flour and cardamom. Carefully fold in blueberries. Spoon mixture over crust to within 2 inches of edge. Fold edge of crust over filling, pleating crust as necessary. In small bowl, beat egg yolk with water. Lightly brush crust edge with egg mixture; sprinkle with sugar.

3 Bake 17 to 23 minutes or until crust is golden brown and filling is bubbly. Cool at least 30 minutes before serving.

1 Serving: Calories 270; Total Fat 9g (Saturated Fat 3.5g, Trans Fat 0g); Cholesterol 35mg; Sodium 180mg; Total Carbohydrate 46g (Dietary Fiber 1g); Protein 2g **Exchanges:** 1 Starch, 2 Other Carbohydrate, 1½ Fat **Carbohydrate Choices:** 3

ginger-lemon-blueberry pie

prep time: 35 Minutes • **start to finish:** 3 Hours 20 Minutes • 8 servings

Crust

- 1 box Pillsbury refrigerated pie crusts, softened as directed on box
- 6 teaspoons sugar
- 1 teaspoon half-and-half

Filling

- 5 cups fresh blueberries
- ½ cup sugar
- 2 tablespoons chopped crystallized ginger
- 2 tablespoons quick-cooking tapioca
- 1 teaspoon grated lemon peel
- 1 tablespoon fresh lemon juice

1 Place foil or cookie sheet on oven rack below middle rack to catch any spills if filling should bubble over during baking. Heat oven to 400°F.

2 Unroll 1 pie crust on work surface. Sprinkle top of crust with 1½ teaspoons of the sugar. With rolling pin, roll lightly to coat with sugar. Place sugared side up in 9-inch glass pie plate, and continue as directed on box for Two-Crust Pie.

3 In large bowl, mix filling ingredients; spoon into crust-lined pie plate. Top with second crust; seal edge and flute. Cut slits in several places in top of pie. Brush top of pie with half-and-half; sprinkle with remaining 4½ teaspoons sugar. Cover edge with foil to prevent excessive browning.

4 Place pie on middle oven rack; bake 35 to 45 minutes or until crust is golden brown and filling is bubbly, removing foil during last 15 minutes of baking. Cool on cooling rack at least 2 hours before serving.

1 Serving: Calories 400; Total Fat 18g (Saturated Fat 4.5g, Trans Fat 3g); Cholesterol 0mg; Sodium 300mg; Total Carbohydrate 57g (Dietary Fiber 3g); Protein 4g **Exchanges:** 1 Starch, 3 Other Carbohydrate, 3½ Fat **Carbohydrate Choices:** 4

three-berry pie

prep time: **20 Minutes** • start to finish: **3 Hours 35 Minutes** • **10 servings**

1 box Pillsbury refrigerated pie crusts, softened as directed on box

1½ cups sugar

5 tablespoons cornstarch

2 tablespoons quick-cooking tapioca

¼ teaspoon salt

3 cups fresh or frozen (thawed and drained) blackberries

2 cups fresh or frozen (thawed and drained) raspberries

2 cups fresh or frozen (thawed and drained) blueberries

1 tablespoon milk

2 teaspoons sugar

1 Place large cookie sheet on oven rack below middle rack to catch any spills if filling should bubble over during baking. Heat oven to 450°F. Make pie crusts as directed on box for Two-Crust Pie, using 9-inch glass pie plate.

2 In large bowl, stir together 1½ cups sugar, the cornstarch, tapioca and salt; add berries, and gently toss. Let stand 15 minutes. Spoon into crust-lined pie plate. Cut second crust into ½-inch-wide strips. Arrange strips in lattice design over filling. Trim and seal edges. Brush crust with milk; sprinkle with 2 teaspoons sugar.

3 Place pie on middle oven rack; bake 15 minutes. Reduce oven temperature to 375°F. Cover crust edge with strips of foil to prevent excessive browning; bake 40 to 45 minutes longer or until crust is golden brown and filling is bubbly. Cool 2 hours before serving.

1 Serving: Calories 366; Total Fat 12g (Saturated Fat 5g, Trans Fat 0g); Cholesterol 5g; Sodium 282mg; Total Carbohydrate 67g (Dietary Fiber 5g); Protein 3g **Exchanges:** 1 Starch, 1 Fruit, 2½ Other Carbohydrate, 2 Fat **Carbohydrate Choices:** 4½

gluten-free peach crumble pie

prep time: 20 Minutes • start to finish: 2 Hours 55 Minutes • 8 servings

1 container Pillsbury Gluten Free refrigerated pie and pastry dough

⅓ cup packed brown sugar

1 teaspoon ground cinnamon

1 can (21 oz) gluten-free peach pie filling with more fruit

Sweetened whipped cream, if desired

1 Heat oven to 425°F. Divide dough in half. In medium bowl, crumble one half into coarse crumbs. Stir in brown sugar and cinnamon. Spread in ungreased 13x9-inch pan. Bake 8 to 10 minutes or until mixture begins to brown. Cool 5 minutes; stir to break up.

2 Meanwhile, knead remaining dough until softened and no longer crumbly. Flatten into a round; place between 2 sheets of cooking parchment or waxed paper. Roll into a round 1½ inches larger than top of 9-inch pie plate.

3 Carefully peel off top sheet of paper. Replace paper to cover loosely; carefully turn dough over, and remove second sheet of paper. Use paper to carefully turn dough over into ungreased pie plate; remove paper. Press dough firmly against bottom and up side of plate. Flatten edge with fork or crimp for decorative edge. Spoon pie filling into crust-lined pie plate.

4 Cover crust edges with strips of foil. Bake 20 minutes. Remove from oven; remove foil strips. Sprinkle topping over pie. Bake 10 to 15 minutes longer or until topping and crust edge are golden brown. Cool completely, about 2 hours. Serve with whipped cream.

1 Serving: Calories 610; Total Fat 34g (Saturated Fat 12g, Trans Fat 0g); Cholesterol 0mg; Sodium 680mg; Total Carbohydrate 75g (Dietary Fiber 2g); Protein 1g **Exchanges:** ½ Starch, ½ Fruit, 4 Other Carbohydrate, 6½ Fat **Carbohydrate Choices:** 5

Easy Success Tip

If you are cooking gluten free, always read labels to make sure each recipe ingredient is gluten free. Products and ingredient sources can change.

rhubarb-strawberry tart

prep time: 20 Minutes • **start to finish:** 3 Hours 20 Minutes • **12 servings**

Crust

1 Pillsbury refrigerated pie crust, softened as directed on box

Filling

2 eggs

¾ cup granulated sugar

3 tablespoons all-purpose flour

¼ teaspoon almond extract

3 cups coarsely sliced fresh rhubarb

2 cups sliced fresh strawberries

Streusel

½ cup packed brown sugar

¼ cup all-purpose flour

¼ teaspoon ground nutmeg

2 tablespoons cold butter, cut into pieces

1 Heat oven to 375°F. Place pie crust in 10-inch tart pan with removable bottom as directed on box for One-Crust Filled Pie. Trim edges if necessary.

2 In large bowl, beat eggs with electric mixer on medium speed until light. Beat in granulated sugar, 3 tablespoons flour and the almond extract until well blended. Alternately layer rhubarb and strawberries in crust-lined pan. Pour egg mixture over fruit.

3 In small bowl, mix brown sugar, ¼ cup flour and the nutmeg. With pastry blender or fork, cut in butter until mixture looks like coarse crumbs. Sprinkle over top.

4 Bake 50 to 60 minutes or until crust is golden brown and filling is set in center. Cool completely on cooling rack, about 2 hours. Remove side of pan; cut tart into wedges. Cover and refrigerate any remaining tart.

1 Serving: Calories 220; Total Fat 8g (Saturated Fat 3g, Trans Fat 0g); Cholesterol 45mg; Sodium 100mg; Total Carbohydrate 37g (Dietary Fiber 1g); Protein 2g **Exchanges:** 1 Starch, 1½ Other Carbohydrate, 1½ Fat **Carbohydrate Choices:** 2½

Easy Success Tip

One 16-ounce bag of frozen unsweetened rhubarb can be substituted for the fresh rhubarb. Don't thaw the rhubarb before making the tart but increase the bake time to 55 to 65 minutes.

coconut cream and blackberry pie

prep time: **30 Minutes** • start to finish: **2 Hours 30 Minutes** • **12 servings**

1 Pillsbury refrigerated pie crust, softened as directed on box

½ cup sugar

¼ cup cornstarch

2 cups half-and-half

4 egg yolks

3 tablespoons butter

1 cup flaked coconut

1 teaspoon vanilla

3 cups fresh blackberries

Sweetened whipped cream or frozen (thawed) whipped topping, if desired

1 Heat oven to 450°F. Make pie crust as directed on box for One-Crust Baked Shell, using 9-inch glass pie plate. Cool completely on cooling rack.

2 Meanwhile, in 2-quart saucepan, mix sugar and cornstarch. In small bowl, beat half-and-half and egg yolks with whisk. Gradually add egg mixture to sugar mixture; heat to boiling over medium heat, stirring constantly. Boil 1 minute; remove from heat. Stir in butter, coconut and vanilla. Press plastic wrap on surface of custard to prevent tough layer from forming on top; refrigerate 30 minutes.

3 Spoon custard in baked pie crust. Top with blackberries and whipped cream. Refrigerate about 2 hours or until set. Cover and refrigerate any remaining pie.

1 Serving: Calories 270; Total Fat 16g (Saturated Fat 9g, Trans Fat 0g); Cholesterol 85mg; Sodium 150mg; Total Carbohydrate 28g (Dietary Fiber 2g); Protein 3g **Exchanges:** 1 Starch, 1 Other Carbohydrate, 3 Fat **Carbohydrate Choices:** 2

Easy Success Tip

Swap the blackberries for another favorite berry, such as fresh blueberries or raspberries.

chocolate gingerbread pie

prep time: 15 Minutes • start to finish: 1 Hour 45 Minutes • 12 servings

1 Pillsbury refrigerated pie crust, softened as directed on box

1 roll (16.5 oz) Pillsbury™ refrigerated chocolate chip cookies

2 eggs

¼ cup unsweetened baking cocoa

¼ cup milk

1 teaspoon ground ginger

¼ cup caramel topping

1 cup whipping cream

¼ cup sugar

½ teaspoon vanilla

Chopped crystallized ginger and chocolate shavings, if desired

1 Heat oven to 375°F. Place pie crust in 9-inch glass pie plate as directed on box for One-Crust Filled Pie.

2 In large bowl, mix cookie dough, eggs, cocoa, milk and ½ teaspoon of the ginger. Beat with electric mixer on medium speed until well mixed. Pour into crust. Bake 25 to 27 minutes or until toothpick inserted in center comes out clean.

3 Use toothpick to prick holes across surface of pie. Spread caramel topping on top of warm pie. Refrigerate about 1 hour or until chilled.

4 In large bowl, beat whipping cream, sugar, vanilla and remaining ½ teaspoon ginger with electric mixer on high speed until stiff peaks form. Spread mixture on top of chilled pie. Garnish with crystallized ginger and chocolate shavings. Cover and refrigerate any remaining pie.

1 Serving: Calories 380; Total Fat 22g (Saturated Fat 10g, Trans Fat 2.5g); Cholesterol 70mg; Sodium 260mg; Total Carbohydrate 43g (Dietary Fiber 0g); Protein 4g **Exchanges:** 1½ Starch, 1½ Other Carbohydrate, 4 Fat **Carbohydrate Choices:** 3

Easy Success Tip

Swap out the caramel topping and use chocolate topping instead for an extra chocolaty twist.

chocolate-avocado pie bites

prep time: 30 Minutes • **start to finish:** 1 Hour • **14 pie bites**

1 box Pillsbury refrigerated pie crusts, softened as directed on box

2 ripe avocados, pitted, peeled

¼ cup unsweetened baking cocoa

¼ cup real maple syrup or maple-flavored syrup

¼ cup milk chocolate chips, melted

1 teaspoon vanilla

Frozen whipped topping, thawed, if desired

1 Heat oven to 425°F. Unroll pie crusts on work surface. With 3½- or 4-inch round cutter, cut 7 rounds from each crust; discard scraps. Fit rounds into 14 ungreased regular-size muffin cups, pressing in gently.

2 Bake about 8 minutes or until edges are golden brown. Cool completely, about 15 minutes.

3 Meanwhile, in food processor, place avocados, cocoa, syrup, chocolate chips and vanilla. Cover; process until smooth. Spoon mixture into pie cups. Refrigerate at least 30 minutes but no longer than 4 hours before serving. Garnish with whipped topping. Cover and refrigerate any remaining bites.

1 Pie Bite: Calories 190; Total Fat 11g (Saturated Fat 4g, Trans Fat 0g); Cholesterol 0mg; Sodium 150mg; Total Carbohydrate 22g (Dietary Fiber 2g); Protein 1g **Exchanges:** ½ Starch, 1 Other Carbohydrate, 2 Fat **Carbohydrate Choices:** 1½

Easy Success Tips

For a pretty garnish, top each bite with a fresh mint leaf before serving.

Make the pastry cups up to a day in advance, and fill just before serving.

sweet and salty cookie pie

prep time: 15 Minutes • **start to finish:** 1 Hour 20 Minutes • **12 servings**

1   Pillsbury refrigerated pie crust, softened as directed on box

⅓   cup chocolate-flavored hazelnut spread

½   cup miniature semisweet chocolate chips

½   package (12 cookies) Pillsbury™ Ready to Bake!™ refrigerated sugar cookies

½   cup toffee bits

¼   teaspoon coarse (kosher or sea) salt

1 Heat oven to 350°F. Unroll pie crust on ungreased cookie sheet; prick generously with fork.

2 Bake 5 minutes. Spread chocolate hazelnut spread evenly over crust to within ¼ inch of edge. Sprinkle with chocolate chips.

3 Cut sugar cookies in half horizontally. Place over chocolate hazelnut spread, ½ inch from edge and about 1 inch apart. Sprinkle with toffee bits and salt. Bake 20 to 25 minutes or until pie crust edges are golden brown. Cool 30 minutes; cut into wedges.

1 Serving: Calories 300; Total Fat 17g (Saturated Fat 7g, Trans Fat 0g); Cholesterol 0mg; Sodium 190mg; Total Carbohydrate 35g (Dietary Fiber 0g); Protein 1g **Exchanges:** ½ Starch, 2 Other Carbohydrate, 3½ Fat **Carbohydrate Choices:** 2

dulce de leche pie cups

prep time: **10 Minutes** • start to finish: **40 Minutes** • **14 pie cups**

1 box Pillsbury refrigerated pie crusts, softened as directed on box

3 tablespoons sugar

1 teaspoon ground cinnamon

½ cup canned dulce de leche (caramelized sweetened condensed milk)

3½ cups caramel ice cream

Caramel topping, if desired

1 Heat oven to 425°F. Unroll pie crusts on work surface. With 3½- or 4-inch round cutter, cut 7 rounds from each crust; discard scraps. In small bowl, mix sugar and cinnamon. Dip both sides of rounds into cinnamon-sugar to coat. Fit rounds into 14 ungreased regular-size muffin cups, pressing in gently.

2 Bake about 8 minutes or until edges are golden brown. Cool completely, about 15 minutes.

3 Place heaping teaspoonful dulce de leche in center of each cooled pie cup. Top with a scoop of ice cream. Top with caramel topping. Serve immediately, or store in freezer up to 30 minutes before serving.

1 Pie Cup: Calories 230; Total Fat 11g (Saturated Fat 6g, Trans Fat 0g); Cholesterol 20mg; Sodium 190mg; Total Carbohydrate 30g (Dietary Fiber 0g); Protein 2g **Exchanges:** ½ Starch, 1½ Other Carbohydrate, 2 Fat **Carbohydrate Choices:** 2

Easy Success Tips

Use vanilla ice cream in place of the caramel ice cream, or even a little of both would be fun!

Store any remaining pie cups tightly covered in the freezer for up to 3 days. Thaw slightly before serving.

decadent chocolate-hazelnut tart

prep time: 30 Minutes • start to finish: 1 Hour 30 Minutes • 12 servings

1 Pillsbury refrigerated pie crust, softened as directed on box

2 cups whipping cream

8 oz semisweet baking chocolate

1 cup mascarpone cheese

½ cup chocolate-flavored hazelnut spread

4 egg yolks

1¼ cups toasted hazelnuts

Easy Success Tip

Hazelnuts can be purchased toasted. But if they are not available at your grocery store, toast hazelnuts by spreading in an ungreased shallow pan. Bake at 350°F for 6 to 10 minutes, stirring occasionally, until light brown. If desired, rub the hazelnuts to remove some of the skin.

1 Heat oven to 450°F. Unroll pie crust; place in ungreased 10-inch tart pan with removable bottom. Press crust firmly against bottom and side of pan; trim edges. Bake 8 to 12 minutes or until light golden brown. Remove from oven to cooling rack. If crust puffs in center, flatten gently with back of wooden spoon. Cool 15 minutes.

2 Meanwhile, in 2-quart saucepan, heat ¾ cup of the cream over medium heat until bubbles begin to form around side of pan. DO NOT BOIL. Remove from heat. Stir in chocolate until melted. Stir in ¼ cup of the mascarpone cheese and 6 tablespoons of the hazelnut spread until well blended.

3 In small bowl, beat egg yolks with fork. Gradually add about one-fourth of the melted chocolate mixture to the egg yolks, stirring constantly. Stir egg mixture back into the pan of hot chocolate cream. Cook over medium-low heat, stirring constantly 3 to 5 minutes until mixture begins to thicken; remove from heat. Spread ½ cup of the chocolate mixture in bottom of cooled crust. Press 1 cup of the toasted hazelnuts into hot filling. Carefully spoon remaining chocolate filling over nuts. Refrigerate at least 1 hour until completely cooled.

4 In medium bowl, beat remaining 1¼ cups cream with electric mixer on high speed until slightly thickened. Slowly add the remaining ¾ cup mascarpone cheese and the remaining 2 tablespoons hazelnut spread. Continue beating until stiff peaks form. Pipe or spoon whipped cream mixture over top of cooled tart. Finely chop remaining ¼ cup hazelnuts; sprinkle over whipped cream. Store covered in refrigerator.

1 Serving: Calories 520; Total Fat 44g (Saturated Fat 21g, Trans Fat 1g); Cholesterol 140mg; Sodium 115mg; Total Carbohydrate 25g (Dietary Fiber 2g); Protein 5g **Exchanges:** 1 Starch, ½ Milk, 8 Fat **Carbohydrate Choices:** 1½

gluten-free chocolate tarts

prep time: 25 Minutes • start to finish: 1 Hour 25 Minutes • 12 tarts

½ container Pillsbury Gluten Free refrigerated pie and pastry dough

1½ cups milk

1 box (4-serving size) chocolate pudding and pie filling mix (not instant)

1 cup semisweet chocolate chips

¾ cup frozen whipped topping, thawed, or sweetened whipped cream

Fresh raspberries, chopped chocolate chips or mint leaves, if desired

1 Heat oven to 425°F. Knead dough until softened and no longer crumbly. Press about 1½ tablespoons dough in bottom and up side of each of 12 ungreased regular-size muffin cups. Prick bottoms several times with fork.

2 Bake 5 minutes. Remove from oven; prick bottoms with fork. Bake 5 to 7 minutes longer or until edges are golden brown. Cool 5 minutes; carefully remove from muffin pan to cooling rack. Cool completely, about 20 minutes.

3 Meanwhile, in 2-quart saucepan, stir together milk and pudding mix; cook over medium heat as directed on box. Reduce heat to low; stir in chocolate chips. Continue cooking, stirring until chocolate is melted and mixture is smooth. Remove from heat; cool 15 minutes.

4 Spoon about 2 tablespoons filling into each cooled shell. Refrigerate at least 30 minutes to chill. Top each with 1 tablespoon whipped topping. Garnish with raspberries.

1 Tart: Calories 300; Total Fat 17g (Saturated Fat 8g, Trans Fat 0g); Cholesterol 0mg; Sodium 280mg; Total Carbohydrate 34g (Dietary Fiber 1g); Protein 2g **Exchanges:** ½ Starch, 2 Other Carbohydrate, 3½ Fat **Carbohydrate Choices:** 2

Easy Success Tips

If you love mint and chocolate, stir ½ teaspoon peppermint extract into the pudding mixture. Sprinkle coarsely chopped unwrapped thin rectangular crème de menthe chocolate candies over the whipped topping.

If you are cooking gluten free, always read labels to make sure each recipe ingredient is gluten free. Products and ingredient sources can change.

Easy as Pie with Refrigerated Pie Crust

Making a delicious pie, sweet or savory, has never been so easy or delicious as it is when you use refrigerated pie crusts. Just follow the directions on the package and you'll be serving up slices of your favorite pie in no time—and with little effort! The following tips will help you create perfection every time!

- Keep the crusts in the package in the refrigerator until it is time to use them—you'll want to allow about 15 minutes at room temperature for the crusts to soften.

- For the best quality, use refrigerated pie crusts before the "use-by" date on the package. The crusts can be frozen for up to two months if placed in the freezer before the "use-by" date.

- Start with the right size pie pan—the crusts are designed for an 8- or 9-inch pie plate or pan, or a 10-inch tart pan. Be sure to follow directions in the recipe for the correct size too. A pie plate or pan that is too small may cause the filling to bubble over during baking.

- Always bring the crust to room temperature before making your pie. Let the pouch stand at room temperature 15 minutes, or microwave on Defrost 10 to 20 seconds. If crust is frozen, let the pouch stand at room temperature 60 to 90 minutes before unrolling. Do not microwave frozen crust.

- Slowly and gently unroll the pie crust into the pie plate, then press firmly against the side and bottom of the pie plate. Be careful not to stretch the crust. Follow recipe directions for the pie you are using.

- To prevent over browning, cover the edges with a pie ring or strips of foil after the first 15 minutes of baking or as directed in the recipe.

Top Crust Trivia

For pie crusts that shine, shimmer or glaze, try one of the following top crust ideas.

- For a shiny crust, brush with about 1 tablespoon milk before baking.

- For a crispy sugared crust, brush with about 1 tablespoon water or milk and sprinkle with 1 tablespoon granulated sugar before baking.

- For a glazed crust, brush with a beaten egg or egg white before baking.

raspberry-kissed chocolate-almond crostata

prep time: 20 Minutes • **start to finish:** 2 Hours • 8 servings

Crostata

- 1 can (8 oz) or 1 package (7 oz) almond paste
- 3 tablespoons butter, softened
- 1 egg white
- 3 oz semisweet baking chocolate, melted
- 1 Pillsbury refrigerated pie crust, softened as directed on box
- 2 tablespoons seedless red raspberry jam
- ¼ cup sliced almonds

Garnishes

- 1 teaspoon powdered sugar
- 1 cup whipped cream

1 Heat oven to 375°F. Spray large cookie sheet with cooking spray, or line with cooking parchment paper.

2 Into medium bowl, break up almond paste; add butter and egg white. Beat with electric mixer on medium speed until smooth. Beat in melted chocolate until well blended. (Or, in food processor bowl with metal blade, break up almond paste; add butter and egg white. Cover; process with on-and-off pulses until smooth. Add melted chocolate. Cover; process until smooth.)

3 Unroll pie crust; place on center of cookie sheet. Spoon almond filling onto middle of crust; spread evenly to within 1½ to 2 inches of edge. Fold edge of crust over filling, forming pleats; press down slightly. Spread jam over filling. Sprinkle almonds over filling and crust.

4 Bake 25 to 35 minutes or until crust is golden brown. Cool completely, about 1 hour. Garnish top with light sprinkling of powdered sugar and dollops of whipped cream.

1 Serving: Calories 430; Total Fat 28g (Saturated Fat 11g, Trans Fat 0g); Cholesterol 30mg; Sodium 160mg; Total Carbohydrate 40g (Dietary Fiber 2g); Protein 5g **Exchanges:** 1½ Starch, 1 Other Carbohydrate, 5½ Fat **Carbohydrate Choices:** 2½

hazelnut–macchiato mocha pie

prep time: 25 Minutes • **start to finish:** 2 Hours • 8 servings

1 Pillsbury refrigerated pie crust, softened as directed on box

1 box (6-serving size) chocolate instant pudding and pie filling mix

1 tablespoon instant coffee granules

1¼ cups plus whole milk

½ cup hazelnut-flavored liquid nondairy creamer

2 cups frozen whipped topping, thawed

¾ cup mocha cappuccino-flavored hazelnut spread

1 tablespoon mocha cappuccino–flavored hazelnut spread

1 teaspoon whole milk

1 Heat oven to 450°F. Make pie crust as directed on box for One-Crust Baked Shell using 9-inch glass pie plate. Cool completely, about 30 minutes.

2 Meanwhile, in large bowl, mix pudding mix and coffee granules. Add 1¼ cups of the milk and the nondairy creamer; beat with whisk 2 minutes. Refrigerate.

3 In medium bowl, beat 1 cup of the whipped topping and ¼ cup of the mocha cappuccino spread with whisk until blended. Refrigerate.

4 Spread ½ cup of the mocha cappuccino spread in bottom of cooled pie crust. Carefully layer and spread the pudding mixture, the mocha whipped topping mixture and the remaining 1 cup whipped topping in pie.

5 In small microwavable bowl, mix remaining 1 tablespoon mocha cappuccino spread and remaining 1 teaspoon milk. Microwave uncovered on High 15 to 20 seconds or until melted; stir. Drizzle over pie. Refrigerate 1 hour before serving. Cover and refrigerate any remaining pie.

1 Serving: Calories 440; Total Fat 24g (Saturated Fat 9g, Trans Fat 0g); Cholesterol 5mg; Sodium 370mg; Total Carbohydrate 52g (Dietary Fiber 1g); Protein 4g **Exchanges:** 1½ Starch, 2 Other Carbohydrate, 4½ Fat **Carbohydrate Choices:** 3½

candy bar tarts

prep time: 20 Minutes • **start to finish:** 3 Hours 40 Minutes • 24 tarts

Crust

- 1 **box Pillsbury refrigerated pie crusts, softened as directed on box**

Filling

- 2 **bars (2.07 oz each) milk chocolate–covered peanut, caramel and nougat candy**
- 4 **oz (half of 8-oz package) cream cheese, softened**
- 2 **tablespoons plus 2 teaspoons sugar**
- 1 **egg**
- 2 **tablespoons sour cream**
- 2 **tablespoons creamy peanut butter**

Topping

- 1 **tablespoon whipping cream**
- ¼ **cup milk chocolate chips**

1 Heat oven to 450°F. Unroll pie crusts on work surface. With rolling pin, roll each crust lightly into 12-inch round. With 3-inch round cutter, cut 24 rounds from crusts, rerolling scraps as necessary. Press 1 pie crust round in bottom and up side of each of 24 ungreased mini muffin cups, so edges of crusts extend slightly above sides of cups. Bake 5 to 7 minutes or until very light golden brown; cool. Reduce oven temperature to 325°F.

2 Cut candy bars in half lengthwise; cut into ⅛-inch pieces; chop coarsely. Place candy bar pieces in bottoms of crust-lined cups, reserving some for garnish. In small bowl, beat cream cheese and sugar with electric mixer on medium speed until smooth. Beat in egg until well blended. Add sour cream and peanut butter, beating until mixture is smooth. Spoon 2 teaspoons cream cheese mixture over candy bar pieces in each tart.

3 Bake at 325°F 20 to 22 minutes or until center is set. Cool completely, about 30 minutes.

4 In 1-quart saucepan, heat whipping cream until very warm. Remove from heat; stir in chocolate chips until melted and smooth. Spread over top of each tart. Garnish with reserved candy bar pieces. Refrigerate 2 to 3 hours before serving. Cover and refrigerate any remaining tarts.

1 Tart: Calories 150; Total Fat 9g (Saturated Fat 4g, Trans Fat 0g); Cholesterol 20mg; Sodium 110mg; Total Carbohydrate 15g (Dietary Fiber 0g); Protein 1g **Exchanges:** ½ Starch, ½ Other Carbohydrate, 2 Fat **Carbohydrate Choices:** 1

gluten-free pecan pie

prep time: 20 Minutes • **start to finish:** 3 Hours 5 Minutes • 8 servings

Crust

½ container Pillsbury Gluten Free refrigerated pie and pastry dough

Filling

⅔ cup sugar

⅓ cup butter, melted

1 cup corn syrup

3 eggs

1 cup pecan halves or broken pecans

Sweetened whipped cream, if desired

1 Heat oven to 375°F. Knead dough until softened and no longer crumbly. Flatten into a round; place between 2 sheets of cooking parchment or waxed paper. Roll into a round 1½ inches larger than top of 9-inch pie plate.

2 Carefully peel off top sheet of paper. Replace paper to cover loosely; carefully turn dough over, and remove second sheet of paper. Use paper to carefully turn dough over into ungreased pie plate; remove paper. Press dough firmly against bottom and up side of plate. Flatten edge with fork or crimp for decorative edge.

3 In medium bowl, beat sugar, melted butter, corn syrup and eggs with whisk or hand beater until well blended. Stir in pecans. Pour into crust-lined pie plate. Cover edge of crust with strips of foil.

4 Bake 40 to 50 minutes or until center is set, removing foil for last 15 minutes of bake time. Cool 30 minutes. Refrigerate at least 2 hours or until chilled. Serve with whipped cream. Cover and refrigerate any remaining pie.

1 Serving: Calories 630; Total Fat 36g (Saturated Fat 12g, Trans Fat 0g); Cholesterol 90mg; Sodium 460mg; Total Carbohydrate 74g (Dietary Fiber 1g); Protein 4g **Exchanges:** 1½ Starch, 3½ Other Carbohydrate, 7 Fat **Carbohydrate Choices:** 5

Easy Success Tip

If you are cooking gluten free, always read labels to make sure each recipe ingredient is gluten free. Products and ingredient sources can change.

gluten-free maple-walnut pumpkin pie

prep time: 25 Minutes • **start to finish:** 4 Hours 50 Minutes • 8 servings

Crust and Filling

- ½ container Pillsbury Gluten Free refrigerated pie and pastry dough
- 2 eggs
- 1 teaspoon pumpkin pie spice
- 1 can (15 oz) pumpkin (not pumpkin pie mix)
- 1 can (14 oz) sweetened condensed milk (not evaporated)
- 3 tablespoons real maple syrup or gluten-free maple-flavored syrup

Topping

- ⅓ cup packed brown sugar
- ⅓ cup chopped walnuts
- 1 tablespoon butter, softened

Maple Whipped Cream

- 1 cup whipping cream
- ¼ cup real maple syrup or gluten-free maple-flavored syrup

1 Heat oven to 425°F. Knead dough until softened and no longer crumbly. Flatten into a round; place between 2 sheets of cooking parchment or waxed paper. Roll into a round 1½ inches larger than top of 9-inch pie plate.

2 Carefully peel off top sheet of paper. Replace paper to cover loosely; carefully turn dough over, and remove second sheet of paper. Use paper to carefully turn dough over into ungreased pie plate; remove paper. Press dough firmly against bottom and up side of plate. Flatten edge with fork or crimp for decorative edge.

3 In medium bowl, beat eggs slightly with whisk. Beat in pumpkin pie spice, pumpkin, condensed milk and syrup. Pour into crust-lined pie plate. Cover edge of crust with strips of foil.

4 Bake 15 minutes. Reduce oven temperature to 350°F. Bake 30 minutes longer. Meanwhile, in small bowl, mix topping ingredients until crumbly. Sprinkle over top of pie. Bake about 10 minutes longer or until knife inserted in center comes out clean. Cool 30 minutes. Refrigerate about 3 hours or until chilled.

5 Just before serving, in large bowl, beat cream with electric mixer on medium speed about 1 minute or until cream begins to thicken, then on high speed until soft peaks form. Gradually beat in syrup until blended and stiff peaks form. Serve with pie. Cover and refrigerate any remaining pie and whipped cream.

1 Serving: Calories 550; Total Fat 27g (Saturated Fat 10g, Trans Fat 0g); Cholesterol 65mg; Sodium 440mg; Total Carbohydrate 69g (Dietary Fiber 2g); Protein 7g **Exchanges:** 1 Starch, 3 Other Carbohydrate, ½ Low-Fat Milk, 5 Fat **Carbohydrate Choices:** 4½

ginger-praline pumpkin tart

prep time: 15 Minutes • start to finish: 2 Hours 5 Minutes • 10 servings

Crust

- 1 Pillsbury refrigerated pie crust, softened as directed on box
- ⅓ cup chopped glazed pecans (from 5-oz bag)
- 1 tablespoon chopped crystallized ginger

Filling

- 2 eggs
- ½ cup sugar
- 1 teaspoon ground cinnamon
- ¾ cup whipping cream
- 1 can (15 oz) pumpkin (not pumpkin pie mix)

Garnish

- ⅓ cup chopped glazed pecans (from 5-oz bag)
- 2 tablespoons chopped crystallized ginger
- ½ cup whipping cream, whipped

1 Place cookie sheet in oven on middle oven rack; heat oven to 425°F. Place pie crust in 10-inch tart pan with removable bottom as directed on box for One-Crust Filled Pie.

2 Sprinkle ⅓ cup pecans and 1 tablespoon ginger in bottom of crust; press in lightly. Place tart pan on preheated cookie sheet in oven. Bake 8 to 10 minutes or until set but not browned. Remove cookie sheet with pan from oven.

3 Meanwhile, in large bowl, mix filling ingredients until well blended. Pour into partially baked crust.

4 Return cookie sheet and pan to oven. Reduce oven temperature to 350°F; bake 45 to 50 minutes or until knife inserted in center comes out clean. Cool on cooling rack 1 hour before serving.

5 In small bowl, mix ⅓ cup pecans and 2 tablespoons ginger. Top each serving with whipped cream and 1 tablespoon pecan mixture.

1 Serving: Calories 340; Total Fat 17g (Saturated Fat 8g, Trans Fat 0g); Cholesterol 80mg; Sodium 140mg; Total Carbohydrate 42g (Dietary Fiber 1g); Protein 3g **Exchanges:** 1 Starch, 2 Other Carbohydrate, 3½ Fat **Carbohydrate Choices:** 3

raspberry-filled jelly doughnuts

prep time: 30 Minutes • start to finish: 30 Minutes • 10 doughnuts

6 tablespoons butter, melted

¾ cup sugar

¾ teaspoon ground cinnamon

⅓ cup raspberry jelly

1 can (12 oz) Pillsbury Grands! Jr. Golden Layers refrigerated buttermilk biscuits (10 biscuits)

1 Heat oven to 375°F. In small bowl, place melted butter. In another small bowl, mix sugar and cinnamon; set aside. Stir jelly until smooth. Seal tip of large baster with foil. Remove rubber bulb. Spoon jelly into baster; replace bulb.

2 Bake biscuits as directed on can. Immediately dip each hot biscuit into melted butter, coating all sides. Roll in sugar mixture, heavily coating all sides of each biscuit. Remove foil from tip of baster. Insert baster in side of each biscuit; squeeze small amount of jelly into center. (Refill baster as needed.) Serve warm or cool.

1 Doughnut: Calories 240; Total Fat 11g (Saturated Fat 2g, Trans Fat 0g); Cholesterol 0mg; Sodium 370mg; Total Carbohydrate 34g (Dietary Fiber 1g); Protein 2g **Exchanges:** 1 Starch, 1 Fruit, 2 Fat **Carbohydrate Choices:** 3

Easy Success Tip

To reheat the doughnuts, wrap them loosely in foil. Heat at 350°F for 5 to 10 minutes or until warm.

baked sugar doughnuts

prep time: 10 Minutes • start to finish: 30 Minutes • 8 servings (1 doughnut and 1 center each)

1 can (16.3 oz) Pillsbury Grands! refrigerated biscuits (8 biscuits)

¾ cup sugar

¾ teaspoon ground cinnamon

⅓ cup butter, melted

1 Heat oven to 350°F. Separate dough into 8 biscuits. Place biscuits on work surface. With 1¼-inch round cutter, cut hole in center of each.

2 In bowl, mix sugar and cinnamon. Dip all sides of biscuits and centers into butter; shake off excess butter. Coat with cinnamon-sugar. Place on ungreased large cookie sheet.

3 Bake 14 to 18 minutes or until golden brown.

1 Serving: Calories 320; Total Fat 15g (Saturated Fat 6g, Trans Fat 4g); Cholesterol 20mg; Sodium 630mg; Total Carbohydrate 44g (Dietary Fiber 0g); Protein 3g **Exchanges:** 1 Starch, 2 Other Carbohydrate, 3 Fat **Carbohydrate Choices:** 3

Easy Success Tip

To reheat, place 1 doughnut at a time on a microwavable plate. Microwave uncovered on Medium (50%) for 10 to 20 seconds or just until warm.

apple-filled cinnamon-sugar doughnuts

prep time: 20 Minutes • start to finish: 40 Minutes • 8 doughnuts

1 can (16.3 oz) Pillsbury Grands! Flaky Layers refrigerated original biscuits (8 biscuits)

1 Granny Smith apple, peeled and cored

⅓ cup sugar

1 teaspoon ground cinnamon

2 tablespoons butter, melted

Caramel topping, if desired

1 Heat oven to 350°F. Spray cookie sheet with cooking spray.

2 Separate dough into 8 biscuits. Press or roll each to form 5-inch round. Cut apple into 8 (¼-inch) rings. Place 1 apple ring on center of each biscuit. In small bowl, mix sugar and cinnamon. Sprinkle about 1 teaspoon cinnamon-sugar over each apple ring.

3 Wrap biscuit around each apple ring to cover completely, pinching ends together to form tight seal. Place biscuits, sealed side down, on cookie sheet.

4 Bake 18 to 22 minutes or until biscuits are deep golden brown. Brush tops of biscuits with melted butter, and sprinkle with remaining cinnamon-sugar. Drizzle with caramel topping. Serve immediately.

1 Doughnut: Calories 250; Total Fat 11g (Saturated Fat 4g, Trans Fat 2g); Cholesterol 10mg; Sodium 570mg; Total Carbohydrate 36g (Dietary Fiber 0g); Protein 3g **Exchanges:** 1 Starch, 1½ Other Carbohydrate, 2 Fat **Carbohydrate Choices:** 2½

Easy Success Tips

Sprinkle the doughnuts with powdered sugar instead of the cinnamon-sugar for a fun variation.

These doughnuts taste best straight out of the oven. To make up to 2 hours ahead, prepare as directed up to the baking step, then cover and refrigerate until ready to bake. When ready, uncover and bake as directed.

cranberry-orange baklava pinwheels

prep time: 20 Minutes • **start to finish:** 35 Minutes • 20 pinwheels

1 box Pillsbury refrigerated pie crusts, softened as directed on box

2 tablespoons butter, melted

1¼ cups sweetened dried cranberries (6 oz)

1 cup chopped pecans

½ cup sugar

2 teaspoons ground cinnamon

1 tablespoon grated orange peel

1 egg

2 tablespoons water

½ cup honey

1 Heat oven to 400°F. Line cookie sheet with cooking parchment paper, or lightly spray with cooking spray. Unroll pie crusts on work surface; press each into 10½-inch square. Brush squares with melted butter.

2 In food processor, place cranberries, pecans, sugar, cinnamon and orange peel. Cover; process using quick on-and-off motions until mixture is finely chopped. Spread half of mixture on each pie crust square.

3 Roll up each pie crust into a log; pinch edge tightly to seal. In small bowl, beat egg and water until blended. Brush egg mixture over each log. Using serrated knife, cut each log into 10 slices. Place slices cut side up 1 inch apart on cookie sheet, replacing any filling. Reshape slices if necessary.

4 Bake 12 to 15 minutes or until golden brown. Immediately remove parchment paper with pinwheels from cookie sheet to cooling rack. Spoon about 1 teaspoon honey on each slice. Serve warm or cool.

1 Pinwheel: Calories 210; Total Fat 10g (Saturated Fat 3g, Trans Fat 0g); Cholesterol 15mg; Sodium 115mg; Total Carbohydrate 29g (Dietary Fiber 1g); Protein 1g **Exchanges:** ½ Starch, 1½ Other Carbohydrate, 2 Fat **Carbohydrate Choices:** 2

chocolate-orange pastries

prep time: 15 Minutes • **start to finish:** 50 Minutes • 16 pastries

1 package (3 oz) cream cheese, softened

2 to 3 teaspoons grated orange peel

1 Pillsbury refrigerated pie crust, softened as directed on box

¼ cup orange marmalade

½ cup dark chocolate chips

1 egg, beaten

2 teaspoons sugar

1 Heat oven to 350°F. Line cookie sheet with cooking parchment paper, or spray with cooking spray.

2 In small bowl, stir cream cheese and orange peel until blended. Unroll pie crust on work surface. Spread cream cheese mixture evenly over crust.

3 In small microwavable bowl, microwave marmalade uncovered on High 10 seconds. Brush marmalade evenly over cream cheese mixture. Cut crust into 16 wedges, using knife or pizza cutter. Sprinkle chocolate chips evenly over wedges.

4 Roll up each wedge, starting at shortest side and rolling to opposite point. Place pastries point side down on cookie sheet. Brush egg on tops and sides of pastries. Sprinkle evenly with sugar.

5 Bake 20 to 25 minutes or until light golden brown. Remove from cookie sheet to cooling rack. Cool at least 10 minutes before serving.

1 Pastry: Calories 120; Total Fat 7g (Saturated Fat 3g, Trans Fat 0g); Cholesterol 20mg; Sodium 95mg; Total Carbohydrate 14g (Dietary Fiber 0g); Protein 1g **Exchanges:** 1 Starch, 1 Fat **Carbohydrate Choices:** 1

Easy Success Tip

When grating an orange or any other citrus fruit, only grate the outer peel, not the white pith, which can be bitter.

fruit pastry sticks

prep time: **15 Minutes** • start to finish: **40 Minutes** • **18 servings**

1 **Pillsbury refrigerated pie crust, softened as directed on box**

1½ **rolls chewy fruit-flavored snacks in three-foot rolls, any flavor (from 4.5-oz box)**

2 **tablespoons colored sugar**

1 Heat oven to 425°F. Line cookie sheet with cooking parchment paper. Unroll dough; roll or press to 12-inch round. Cut into 9 (1¼-inch) strips. Cut ends as needed so all are straight. Cut strips in half crosswise to make 18 (1¼x4½-inch) strips.

2 Unroll fruit snack. With scissors, cut a total of 18 (about 4-inch-long) pieces. Place 1 piece on each pie crust strip. Fold dough lengthwise over fruit snack; pinch long edges to seal. Twist ends of dough strip in opposite directions. Place on cookie sheet, pressing ends down to seal.

3 Brush top and side of each stick with water; sprinkle with colored sugar.

4 Bake 8 to 10 minutes or until golden brown. Immediately remove from cookie sheet to cooling rack. Cool 5 minutes before serving.

1 Serving: Calories 60; Total Fat 2.5g (Saturated Fat 1g, Trans Fat 0g); Cholesterol 0mg; Sodium 60mg; Total Carbohydrate 8g (Dietary Fiber 0g); Protein 0g **Exchanges:** ½ Other Carbohydrate, ½ Fat **Carbohydrate Choices:** ½

Easy Success Tips

Have fun! Use different flavors of fruit-flavored snacks or different colored sugars to make this recipe your own.

For the young at heart, serve these as stirrers with glasses of milk. The crust will soften and flavor the milk as you stir.

palmiers

prep time: 15 Minutes • start to finish: 30 Minutes • 16 palmiers

1 can (8 oz) Pillsbury refrigerated crescent dinner rolls (8 rolls) or 1 can (8 oz) Pillsbury Crescent Recipe Creations refrigerated seamless dough sheet

¼ cup granulated sugar

2 tablespoons butter, melted

Coarse sugar

1 Heat oven to 375°F. Line cookie sheet with cooking parchment paper. Separate or cut dough into 4 (7x4-inch) rectangles; if using crescent roll dough, firmly press perforations to seal.

2 Sprinkle 1 tablespoon of the granulated sugar on cutting board. Place 2 of the dough rectangles on sugar; press lightly. Brush top of each rectangle with about 1 tablespoon melted butter; sprinkle with 1 tablespoon sugar. Place 1 rectangle on top of another; tightly roll both short sides of the dough rectangle so they meet in the middle. Repeat with remaining 2 dough rectangles.

3 Using serrated knife, cut each roll into 8 slices. Place slices cut side down 2 inches apart on cookie sheet. Sprinkle with coarse sugar. Press each slightly to flatten.

4 Bake 10 to 13 minutes or until golden brown. Cool 1 minute; remove from cookie sheets. Cool completely before serving.

1 Palmier: Calories 70; Total Fat 3.5g (Saturated Fat 2g, Trans Fat 0g); Cholesterol 0mg; Sodium 125mg; Total Carbohydrate 9g (Dietary Fiber 0g); Protein 0g **Exchanges:** ½ Starch, ½ Fat **Carbohydrate Choices:** ½

Easy Success Tips

Instead of (or in addition to) the granulated sugar, try these variations: cinnamon and sugar or citrus peel and sugar.

Palmiers can be stored in an airtight container at room temperature for up to 4 days. If desired, they can be recrisped in a 300°F oven until heated through, about 5 minutes.

strawberry breakfast crescents

prep time: **15 Minutes** • start to finish: **30 Minutes** • **8 rolls**

1 **can (8 oz) Pillsbury refrigerated crescent dinner rolls (8 rolls)**

4 **rolls strawberry chewy fruit-flavored snacks**

⅔ **cup powdered sugar**

¼ **teaspoon vanilla**

2 **to 3 teaspoons milk**

1 Heat oven to 350°F. Spray cookie sheet with cooking spray. Unroll dough; separate into 8 triangles.

2 Unroll fruit-flavored snacks; cut each diagonally into 2 triangles. Place each fruit snack triangle on 1 dough triangle (fold or tuck each fruit snack so all is on dough). Roll up each dough triangle, starting with shortest side of triangle and rolling to opposite point; place point side down on cookie sheet. Curve into crescent shape.

3 Bake 12 to 15 minutes or until golden brown. Cool 2 minutes; remove from cookie sheet. Meanwhile, in small bowl, mix powdered sugar, vanilla and enough milk until smooth and desired drizzling consistency.

4 Drizzle glaze evenly over warm rolls. Serve warm.

1 Roll: Calories 160; Total Fat 5g (Saturated Fat 1g, Trans Fat 0g); Cholesterol 0mg; Sodium 370mg; Total Carbohydrate 29g (Dietary Fiber 0g); Protein 2g **Exchanges:** 1 Starch, 1 Other Carbohydrate, ½ Fat **Carbohydrate Choices:** 2

magic marshmallow crescent puffs

prep time: 35 Minutes • **start to finish:** 35 Minutes • 16 rolls

Rolls

- ¼ cup granulated sugar
- 2 tablespoons all-purpose flour
- 1 teaspoon ground cinnamon
- 2 cans (8 oz each) Pillsbury refrigerated crescent dinner rolls (16 rolls total)
- 16 large marshmallows
- ¼ cup butter, melted

Glaze

- ½ cup powdered sugar
- ½ teaspoon vanilla
- 2 to 3 teaspoons milk
- ¼ cup chopped nuts

1 Heat oven to 375°F. Spray 16 regular-size muffin cups with cooking spray. In small bowl, mix granulated sugar, flour and cinnamon.

2 Separate dough into 16 triangles. For each roll, dip 1 marshmallow into melted butter; roll in sugar mixture. Place marshmallow on shortest side of triangle. Roll up, starting at shortest side and rolling to opposite point. Completely cover marshmallow with dough; firmly pinch edges to seal. Dip 1 end in remaining butter; place butter side down in muffin cup.

3 Bake 12 to 15 minutes or until golden brown. (Place foil or cookie sheet on rack below muffin cups to guard against spills.) Cool in pan 1 minute. Remove rolls from muffin cups; place on cooling racks set over waxed paper.

4 In small bowl, mix powdered sugar, vanilla and enough milk for desired drizzling consistency. Drizzle glaze over warm rolls. Sprinkle with nuts. Serve warm.

1 Roll: Calories 200; Total Fat 10g (Saturated Fat 4g, Trans Fat 1.5g); Cholesterol 10mg; Sodium 250mg; Total Carbohydrate 25g (Dietary Fiber 0g); Protein 2g **Exchanges:** 1 Starch, ½ Other Carbohydrate, 2 Fat **Carbohydrate Choices:** 1½

cream cheese–raspberry coffee cake

prep time: 30 Minutes • **start to finish:** 1 Hour 5 Minutes • 12 servings

Coffee Cake

- 2 cans (8 oz each) Pillsbury refrigerated crescent dinner rolls (16 rolls total)
- 1 package (8 oz) cream cheese, softened
- ¼ cup granulated sugar
- 2 teaspoons grated orange peel
- 1 teaspoon vanilla
- 1 egg
- 1 pint (2 cups) fresh raspberries
- 1 teaspoon granulated sugar

Glaze

- ½ cup powdered sugar
- 1 tablespoon butter, softened
- 2 teaspoons orange juice

1 Heat oven to 350°F. Spray large cookie sheet or 14-inch pizza pan with cooking spray. Unroll both cans of dough; separate into 16 triangles. Reserve 4 triangles for topping.

2 On cookie sheet, arrange 12 triangles in circle with points toward center, leaving 3-inch hole in center. Press dough to form 14-inch ring; press seams together to seal. Fold outer and center edges up ¼ inch.

3 In medium bowl, mix cream cheese, ¼ cup granulated sugar, the orange peel, vanilla and egg until well blended. Gently stir in raspberries. (Mixture will be thin.)

4 Spoon raspberry mixture evenly over dough. With scissors or pizza cutter, cut each reserved dough triangle lengthwise into thirds. Place 1 teaspoon granulated sugar on work surface. Press each dough strip into sugar. Arrange sugared dough strips, sugar side up, evenly in spoke pattern over filling. Press ends to seal at center and outer edges.

5 Bake 25 to 30 minutes or until golden brown. Cool 10 minutes.

6 In small bowl, mix glaze ingredients until smooth. Drizzle over coffee cake. Serve warm.

1 Serving: Calories 280; Total Fat 16g (Saturated Fat 8g, Trans Fat 2.5g); Cholesterol 40mg; Sodium 360mg; Total Carbohydrate 27g (Dietary Fiber 2g); Protein 5g **Exchanges:** ½ Starch, 1½ Other Carbohydrate, ½ High-Fat Meat, 2½ Fat **Carbohydrate Choices:** 2

Easy Success Tip

Instead of drizzling this coffee cake with the glaze, sprinkle it with powdered sugar just before serving.

easy danish kringle

prep time: 15 Minutes • start to finish: 1 Hour 15 Minutes • 8 servings

1 Pillsbury refrigerated pie crust, softened as directed on box

⅔ cup chopped pecans

⅓ cup packed brown sugar

3 tablespoons butter, softened

½ cup powdered sugar

¼ teaspoon vanilla

2 to 3 teaspoons milk

3 tablespoons chopped pecans, if desired

1 Heat oven to 375°F. Unroll pie crust on ungreased large cookie sheet.

2 In medium bowl, mix ⅔ cup pecans, the brown sugar and butter. Sprinkle on half of pie crust to within ¾ inch of edge. Brush edge with water; fold crust over pecan mixture. Move to center of cookie sheet. Press edges with fork to seal; prick top with fork.

3 Bake 17 to 22 minutes or until golden brown. Cool 5 minutes. In small bowl, mix powdered sugar, vanilla and 2 teaspoons milk. Stir in enough remaining milk until glaze is smooth. Drizzle glaze over kringle; sprinkle with 3 tablespoons pecans. Cool 30 minutes before serving.

1 Serving: Calories 290; Total Fat 18g (Saturated Fat 6g, Trans Fat 0g); Cholesterol 15mg; Sodium 140mg; Total Carbohydrate 31g (Dietary Fiber 0g); Protein 0g **Exchanges:** 2 Other Carbohydrate, 3½ Fat **Carbohydrate Choices:** 2

cinnamon-sugar snackers

prep time: **30 Minutes** • start to finish: **30 Minutes** • **30 to 40 snack chips**

⅔ **cup sugar**

1 **tablespoon ground cinnamon**

1 **can (12 oz) Pillsbury Grands! Jr. Golden Layers refrigerated buttermilk biscuits (10 biscuits)**

⅓ **cup butter, melted**

1 Heat oven to 400°F. Lightly grease 2 cookie sheets.

2 In small shallow bowl, mix sugar and cinnamon. Separate dough into 10 biscuits. Separate each biscuit into 3 to 4 layers. Dip each layer into melted butter; coat both sides with cinnamon-sugar. Place 1 inch apart on cookie sheets.

3 Bake 6 to 8 minutes or until golden brown. Serve warm.

1 Snack Chip: Calories 80; Total Fat 4g (Saturated Fat 1g, Trans Fat 0g); Cholesterol 0mg; Sodium 140mg; Total Carbohydrate 9g (Dietary Fiber 0g); Protein 1g **Exchanges:** ½ Starch, ½ Fat **Carbohydrate Choices:** ½

mini honey-almond-cranberry crostatas

prep time: 30 Minutes • **start to finish:** 55 Minutes • 8 crostatas

⅓ cup water

⅓ cup honey

1¼ cups fresh or frozen whole cranberries

1 Pillsbury refrigerated pie crust, softened as directed on box

3 tablespoons almond paste, softened (from 3½-oz tube)

1½ teaspoons sliced almonds

8 teaspoons honey

1 Heat oven to 425°F. Place cooking parchment paper on cookie sheet. In 1-quart saucepan, heat water and ⅓ cup honey to boiling. Stir in cranberries; reduce heat to medium-low. Cook 10 to 12 minutes, stirring frequently, until berries have popped and mixture is thickened. Cool slightly, about 15 minutes.

2 Meanwhile, unroll crust on work surface. Roll crust out slightly; cut into 8 (4-inch) rounds. Reroll scraps, and cut remaining rounds if necessary. Place rounds on cookie sheet. Discard scraps.

3 Gently press 1 heaping teaspoon almond paste in center of each crust round. Divide cranberry mixture evenly over almond paste. Fold ½ inch of each crust round over filling, pinching slightly so crust lays flat on cranberry mixture. Sprinkle each with almonds.

4 Bake 14 to 16 minutes or until crust is golden brown. Drizzle 1 teaspoon honey over each crostata. If desired, serve warm with ice cream.

1 Crostata: Calories 300; Total Fat 12g (Saturated Fat 4.5g, Trans Fat 0g); Cholesterol 5mg; Sodium 240mg; Total Carbohydrate 44g (Dietary Fiber 1g); Protein 2g **Exchanges:** ½ Starch, 2½ Other Carbohydrate, 2½ Fat **Carbohydrate Choices:** 3

Gluten-Free Double Chocolate
Sandwich Cookies (page 284)

CHAPTER 6

cookies
and
bars

almond café cookies

prep time: 30 Minutes • **start to finish:** 1 Hour 10 Minutes • 2 dozen cookies

2 packages Pillsbury Ready to Bake! refrigerated sugar cookies

8 oz almond paste

1 cup all-purpose flour

2 tablespoons apricot preserves

2 egg whites

1¼ cups sliced almonds

1 Heat oven to 375°F. Line large cookie sheets with cooking parchment paper.

2 In large bowl, break up cookie dough and almond paste. Add flour and preserves; knead until well blended and mixture forms a ball. Pat into 9x6-inch rectangle. Cut into 24 pieces.

3 In small bowl, beat egg whites with fork or whisk until foamy. In another small bowl, place almonds.

4 Shape each dough piece into a ball. Flatten to 3-inch round. Dip 1 flat side into egg whites, coating 1 side only. Place coated side down onto almond slices. Lightly press to coat with almonds. Place 2 inches apart on cookie sheets, almond side up.

5 Bake 13 to 18 minutes or until cookies are light golden brown. Cool on cookie sheets 2 minutes; remove to cooling racks. Cool completely, about 20 minutes. Store in covered container.

1 Cookie: Calories 270; Total Fat 13g (Saturated Fat 3g, Trans Fat 0g); Cholesterol 0mg; Sodium 100mg; Total Carbohydrate 34g (Dietary Fiber 1g); Protein 4g **Exchanges:** 1½ Starch, 1 Other Carbohydrate, 2 Fat **Carbohydrate Choices:** 2

cherry sugar cookie macaroons

prep time: 25 Minutes • **start to finish:** 1 Hour 40 Minutes • 3 dozen cookies

1 roll Pillsbury™ refrigerated sugar cookies

¾ cup chopped macadamia nuts

¾ cup coarsely chopped dried tart cherries

1 bag (7 oz) sweetened flaked coconut (about 2½ cups)

2 teaspoons vanilla

1 cup red tart cherry preserves

1 Heat oven to 350°F. Line large cookie sheets with cooking parchment paper. Let cookie dough stand at room temperature 10 minutes to soften.

2 In medium bowl, break up cookie dough. Add nuts, cherries, coconut and vanilla. Mix with wooden spoon or knead with hands until well blended. Shape rounded tablespoonfuls of dough into balls. Place 2 inches apart on cookie sheets.

3 Bake 15 to 20 minutes or until edges are light golden brown. Cool 3 minutes. With back of teaspoon, make indentation in center of each cookie. Spoon 1 teaspoon preserves in each indentation. Cool completely, about 20 minutes. Store in covered container.

1 Cookie: Calories 140; Total Fat 6g (Saturated Fat 2.5g, Trans Fat 0.5g); Cholesterol 0mg; Sodium 60mg; Total Carbohydrate 20g (Dietary Fiber 0g); Protein 1g **Exchanges:** ½ Starch, 1 Other Carbohydrate, 1 Fat **Carbohydrate Choices:** 1

pumpkin streusel tassies

prep time: 30 Minutes • **start to finish:** 1 Hour 5 Minutes • **2 dozen cookies**

1¼ cups canned pumpkin pie mix (not plain pumpkin)

¼ cup half-and-half

1 egg

¼ cup all-purpose flour

¼ cup packed brown sugar

3 tablespoons quick-cooking or old-fashioned oats

2 tablespoons butter, melted

½ teaspoon ground cinnamon

1 box Pillsbury refrigerated pie crusts, softened as directed on box

1 Heat oven to 425°F. Spray 24 mini muffin cups with cooking spray. In medium bowl, stir pumpkin pie mix, half-and-half and egg until blended; set aside. In small bowl, mix flour, brown sugar, oats, butter and cinnamon; set aside.

2 Unroll pie crusts on work surface. With 3-inch round cutter, cut 12 rounds from each crust. Fit rounds into muffin cups, pressing in gently. Spoon slightly less than 1 tablespoon pumpkin filling into each crust-lined cup; sprinkle each with 2 teaspoons oat topping.

3 Bake 15 to 20 minutes or until puffed and tip of knife inserted in center comes out clean. Immediately run knife around edges of cookies. Remove from pans to cooling rack; cool 15 minutes. Serve warm or cool.

1 Cookie: Calories 82; Total Fat 4g (Saturated Fat 2g, Trans Fat 0g); Cholesterol 20mg; Sodium 76mg; Total Carbohydrate 11g (Dietary Fiber 0g); Protein 1g **Exchanges:** ½ Starch, ½ Other Carbohydrate, ½ Fat **Carbohydrate Choices:** 1

lemon-pistachio-blackberry thumbprints

prep time: 25 Minutes • **start to finish:** 35 Minutes • 3 dozen cookies

1 **roll Pillsbury refrigerated sugar cookies**

½ **cup shelled salted roasted pistachios, chopped**

⅓ **cup all-purpose flour**

1 **teaspoon grated lemon peel**

½ **cup seedless blackberry jam**

1 **cup powdered sugar**

1 **tablespoon honey**

Water

1 Heat oven to 325°F. Line large cookie sheets with cooking parchment paper, or spray with cooking spray. Let cookie dough stand at room temperature 10 minutes to soften.

2 In large bowl, break up cookie dough. Add pistachios, flour and lemon peel. Mix with wooden spoon, or knead with hands until well blended. Shape dough into 36 (1-inch) balls. Place 2 inches apart on cookie sheets. With thumb or handle of wooden spoon, make indentation ¾ inch wide in center of each cookie. Spoon about ½ teaspoon jam into each indentation.

3 Bake 10 to 13 minutes or until set but not browned. Remove to cooling racks. Cool 3 minutes.

4 In small bowl, mix powdered sugar, honey and 1 tablespoon water until smooth. If necessary, stir in water, 1 teaspoon at a time, until of drizzling consistency. Drizzle honey glaze over warm cookies. Store in covered container.

1 Cookie: Calories 90; Total Fat 3g (Saturated Fat 1g, Trans Fat 0.5g); Cholesterol 0mg; Sodium 50mg; Total Carbohydrate 15g (Dietary Fiber 0g); Protein 1g **Exchanges:** ½ Starch, ½ Other Carbohydrate, ½ Fat **Carbohydrate Choices:** 1

Easy Success Tips

To easily fill the center of each cookie, stir the jam thoroughly. Place it in a freezer plastic bag; cut a small hole in one corner. Squeeze the bag to fill.

For ease in cleanup, place cooking parchment paper under the cooling rack before drizzling cookies.

coconut-pecan florentine sandwich cookies

prep time: 30 Minutes • **start to finish:** 1 Hour 5 Minutes • **2 dozen sandwich cookies**

1 roll Pillsbury refrigerated sugar cookies

1 container coconut pecan creamy ready-to-spread frosting

⅔ cup old-fashioned oats

⅛ teaspoon salt

1 cup mocha cappuccino-flavored hazelnut spread

1 Heat oven to 350°F. Line 2 large cookie sheets with cooking parchment paper.

2 Let cookie dough stand at room temperature 10 minutes to soften. In large bowl, break up cookie dough. Add frosting, oats and salt. Beat with electric mixer on medium speed until well blended. Working with half of the dough, drop by rounded tablespoonfuls 3 inches apart onto cookie sheets to make 24 cookies. (Cookies will spread.)

3 Bake 2 cookie sheets at a time, 10 to 14 minutes or until golden brown, turning cookie sheets halfway through bake time. While cookies are baking, drop remaining tablespoonfuls of dough onto cooking parchment paper to make 24 additional cookies. Remove baked cookies and parchment paper to cooling rack. Cool completely, about 10 minutes. Repeat with remaining dough and cooking parchment paper.

4 Spread 1 heaping teaspoon of the hazelnut spread onto bottom of 24 cookies. Top with remaining cookies, bottom side down; press lightly. Store in covered container.

1 Sandwich Cookie: Calories 250; Total Fat 14g (Saturated Fat 4.5g, Trans Fat 2g); Cholesterol 0mg; Sodium 105mg; Total Carbohydrate 30g (Dietary Fiber 0g); Protein 2g **Exchanges:** 1 Starch, 1 Other Carbohydrate, 2½ Fat **Carbohydrate Choices:** 2

Easy Wows for Sandwich Cookies

For delicious specialty cookies that will bring "wow" reviews, try this. Bake up a package of ready-to-bake refrigerated cookies. Spread half of the baked cookies with a filling, then top with the remaining cookies and press together. Here are some easy filling ideas to get you started.

Linzer Cookies: Spread seedless or regular jam between pairs of baked sugar cookies. Sprinkle tops with coarse or powdered sugar. Melt about 1 cup semisweet or dark chocolate with 1 teaspoon shortening and drizzle over tops of cookies.

PB & J Cookies: Mix ⅓ cup creamy vanilla ready-to-spread frosting with 2 tablespoons peanut butter until smooth. Spread between pairs of baked peanut butter cookies with a layer of a favorite jam or jelly.

S'More Cookies: Spread marshmallow creme between pairs of baked chocolate chip cookies. Drizzle tops of cookies with melted milk chocolate candy and sprinkle with a few coarsely crushed graham cracker crumbs.

Cool Cookie-Wiches: Spoon slightly softened ice cream or frozen yogurt between pairs of any flavor baked cookies. Roll edges in chopped nuts, mini chocolate chips, coconut, or colored sprinkles. Wrap in plastic wrap or foil and freeze.

Lemon Delights: Spread purchased lemon curd between pairs of baked sugar cookies. Dip one-half of each sandwich cookie in melted white candy coating.

Chocolate-Nut Cookies: Spread creamy chocolate fudge frosting between pairs of sugar or chocolate chip baked cookies. Roll edges in chopped pecans, walnuts or even chopped maraschino cherries.

gluten-free double chocolate sandwich cookies

prep time: 30 Minutes • start to finish: 1 Hour • 1 dozen sandwich cookies

1 container Pillsbury™ Gluten Free refrigerated chocolate chip cookie dough

2 oz semisweet baking chocolate, melted, cooled

¾ cup fluffy white whipped ready-to-spread frosting

1 Heat oven to 350°F. In medium bowl, break up cookie dough. Knead in chocolate until well blended. Shape rounded tablespoonfuls of dough into balls. On ungreased cookie sheet, place balls 2 inches apart. With bottom of glass, flatten slightly.

2 Bake 10 to 12 minutes or until set. Cool 2 minutes on cookie sheet. Remove from cookie sheet to cooling rack. Cool completely, about 30 minutes.

3 For each sandwich cookie, spread 1 tablespoon frosting on bottom of 1 cookie. Top with second cookie, bottom side down; press together gently.

1 Sandwich Cookie: Calories 260; Total Fat 14g (Saturated Fat 6g, Trans Fat 1.5g); Cholesterol 15mg; Sodium 150mg; Total Carbohydrate 35g (Dietary Fiber 0g); Protein 1g **Exchanges:** ½ Starch, 2 Other Carbohydrate, 2½ Fat **Carbohydrate Choices:** 2

Easy Success Tips

We like the white filling in these sandwich cookies, but if your family loves chocolate, why not substitute chocolate frosting for the white?

If you are cooking gluten free, always read labels to make sure each recipe ingredient is gluten free. Products and ingredient sources can change.

quick snickerdoodles

prep time: 1 Hour • **start to finish:** 1 Hour • 32 cookies

3 tablespoons sugar

½ teaspoon ground cinnamon

1 roll Pillsbury refrigerated sugar cookies

¼ cup all-purpose flour

1 Heat oven to 350°F. In small bowl, mix sugar and cinnamon.

2 In large bowl, break up cookie dough. Stir or knead in flour until well blended. Reshape into log. Cut cookie dough into 32 (¼-inch) slices. Shape each into a ball, and roll in cinnamon-sugar; place 2 inches apart on ungreased cookie sheets.

3 Bake 10 to 14 minutes or until edges are golden brown. Cool 1 minute; remove from cookie sheets to cooling rack.

1 Cookie: Calories 70; Total Fat 2g (Saturated Fat 1g, Trans Fat 1g); Cholesterol 0mg; Sodium 55mg; Total Carbohydrate 12g (Dietary Fiber 0g); Protein 1g **Exchanges:** 1 Other Carbohydrate, ½ Fat **Carbohydrate Choices:** 1

Easy Success Tip

Fill a cellophane bag (from a party or paper store) with these tasty cookies. Tie the top with a metallic star foil garland and a gift card. It's a tasty treat for a shut-in or elderly friend.

coconut cookie blossoms

prep time: 25 Minutes • start to finish: 1 Hour 45 Minutes • 2 dozen cookies

1 package Pillsbury Ready to Bake! refrigerated sugar cookies

¼ cup butter

1 cup sugar

½ cup coconut milk

4 eggs, separated (4 yolks and 3 whites)

½ cup shredded coconut

¼ cup chocolate-flavored hazelnut spread

1 Heat oven to 375°F. Spray 24 mini muffin cups and top of pans with cooking spray. Place 1 cookie dough round in each muffin cup. Bake 15 to 20 minutes or until golden brown. Cool completely in pans, about 20 minutes. Loosen with tip of knife; gently lift out, and place back into muffin cups.

2 While cookie cups are cooling, in 1½-quart saucepan, mix butter, ½ cup of the sugar, the coconut milk and egg yolks with whisk until well blended. Cook on medium-low heat until mixture thickens, stirring constantly. DO NOT BOIL. Stir in coconut; set aside.

3 In medium bowl, beat 3 of the egg whites with electric mixer on high speed until foamy (save remaining egg white for another use). Gradually add remaining ½ cup sugar, 1 tablespoon at a time; beat until stiff peaks form.

4 Spoon warm coconut mixture into cups. Spoon or pipe rounded tablespoon meringue over each cup. Bake 10 to 12 minutes or until meringue is light golden brown. Cool in pans 20 minutes.

5 Meanwhile, in small microwavable bowl, microwave hazelnut spread uncovered on High 15 to 20 seconds or until thin enough to drizzle. Drizzle over meringue. Serve warm or cool. Store in refrigerator.

1 Cookie: Calories 160; Total Fat 8g (Saturated Fat 3.5g, Trans Fat 0g); Cholesterol 35mg; Sodium 80mg; Total Carbohydrate 21g (Dietary Fiber 0g); Protein 1g **Exchanges:** ½ Starch, 1 Other Carbohydrate, 1½ Fat **Carbohydrate Choices:** 1½

chocolate-dipped heart cookies

prep time: 1 Hour • **start to finish:** 1 Hour • 28 cookies

1 roll (16.5 oz) Pillsbury refrigerated sugar cookies

¼ cup all-purpose flour

Additional ¼ cup all-purpose flour for rolling dough

1½ cups semisweet chocolate chips

1 tablespoon shortening

1 Heat oven to 350°F. In large bowl, break up cookie dough. Stir or knead in ¼ cup flour until well blended. Remove half the dough, and refrigerate remaining dough until needed.

2 Sprinkle 2 tablespoons flour onto work surface. With rolling pin, roll dough ⅛ inch thick. With floured 3-inch heart-shaped cookie cutter, cut out dough hearts. Gently brush excess flour from dough hearts. On ungreased cookie sheets, place hearts 2 inches apart. Repeat with remaining dough and 2 tablespoons flour.

3 Bake 7 to 9 minutes or until light golden brown. Cool 1 minute; remove from cookie sheets to cooling racks. Cool completely, about 15 minutes.

4 Place sheet of waxed paper on cookie sheet. In 1-quart saucepan, melt chocolate chips and shortening over low heat, stirring occasionally, until smooth. Remove from heat. Dip half of each cookie into melted chocolate; allow excess to drip off. Place on waxed paper. Refrigerate until set.

1 Cookie: Calories 130 (Calories from Fat 60); Total Fat 7g (Saturated Fat 2.5g, Trans Fat 1g); Cholesterol 5mg; Sodium 55mg; Total Carbohydrate 18g (Dietary Fiber 0g, Sugars 11g); Protein 1g **Exchanges:** ½ Starch, ½ Other Carbohydrate, 1½ Fat **Carbohydrate Choices:** 1

Easy Success Tip

Pillsbury refrigerated chocolate chip cookies can be substituted for Pillsbury refrigerated sugar cookies.

gluten-free candy-filled chocolate chip cookies

prep time: **15 Minutes** • start to finish: **35 Minutes** • **1 dozen cookies**

1 container Pillsbury Gluten Free refrigerated chocolate chip cookie dough

12 round gluten-free chewy caramels in milk chocolate, unwrapped

1 Heat oven to 350°F. Line cookie sheet with cooking parchment paper.

2 For each cookie, shape 2 tablespoons cookie dough around 1 caramel candy, covering completely. Place cookies with thickest part of dough down 2½ inches apart on cookie sheet.

3 Bake 12 to 14 minutes or until golden brown. Cool 2 minutes; remove to cooling rack. Cool completely, about 15 minutes.

1 Cookie: Calories 170; Total Fat 8g (Saturated Fat 3.5g, Trans Fat 0g); Cholesterol 15mg; Sodium 140mg; Total Carbohydrate 24g (Dietary Fiber 0g); Protein 1g **Exchanges:** ½ Starch, 1 Other Carbohydrate, 1½ Fat **Carbohydrate Choices:** 1½

Easy Success Tips

To enjoy these cookies safely, be sure to cool them completely, as caramel candy gets very hot during baking.

If you are cooking gluten free, always read labels to make sure each recipe ingredient is gluten free. Products and ingredient sources can change.

nutty chocolate hot bites

prep time: 15 Minutes • **start to finish:** 1 Hour 15 Minutes • 24 servings

1 package Pillsbury™ Ready to Bake!™ refrigerated chocolate chip cookies

1¼ cups mixed nuts with peanuts

1¼ cups dark chocolate chips

1¼ cups marshmallow creme

2 tablespoons half-and-half

⅛ teaspoon ground red pepper (cayenne)

1 Heat oven to 375°F. Place paper baking cup in each of 24 regular-size muffin cups. Place 1 cookie dough round in each cup. Using floured fingers, press dough to flatten slightly.

2 Bake 7 to 10 minutes or until golden brown. Cool 15 minutes. Remove from pans to cooling racks. Cool completely, about 20 minutes.

3 Meanwhile, remove Brazil nuts from mixed nuts; coarsely chop Brazil nuts. In 2-quart saucepan, heat chocolate chips, marshmallow creme, half-and-half and red pepper over medium-high heat, stirring occasionally, until chips are melted and mixture is smooth. Stir in Brazil nuts and remaining mixed nuts.

4 Drop about 1 tablespoon nut mixture onto each cookie. Let stand about 15 minutes or until chocolate is set. To serve, remove bites from paper baking cups. If desired, place each bite into a new paper baking cup.

1 Cookie: Calories 200; Total Fat 11g (Saturated Fat 3.5g, Trans Fat 1g); Cholesterol 0mg; Sodium 80mg; Total Carbohydrate 23g (Dietary Fiber 1g); Protein 2g **Exchanges:** ½ Starch, 1 Other Carbohydrate, 2 Fat **Carbohydrate Choices:** 1½

gluten-free chocolate chip peanut butter cups

prep time: 20 Minutes • start to finish: 1 Hour 45 Minutes • 2 dozen cookies

1 container Pillsbury Gluten Free refrigerated chocolate chip cookie dough

24 gluten-free miniature chocolate-covered peanut butter cup candies, unwrapped

1 Heat oven to 350°F. Place mini paper baking cup in each of 24 mini muffin cups. Spray paper baking cups with cooking spray.

2 Place 1 level measuring tablespoonful cookie dough in each paper baking cup.

3 Bake 10 to 12 minutes or until dark golden brown. Immediately press peanut butter cup candy into center of each cookie cup. Cool 5 minutes; remove to cooling rack. Cool 10 minutes. Refrigerate until set, about 1 hour.

1 Cookie: Calories 120; Total Fat 6g (Saturated Fat 2.5g, Trans Fat 0g); Cholesterol 5mg; Sodium 95mg; Total Carbohydrate 15g (Dietary Fiber 0g); Protein 1g **Exchanges:** ½ Starch, ½ Other Carbohydrate, 1 Fat **Carbohydrate Choices:** 1

Easy Success Tips

Dress up these tasty treats for a special occasion by topping each with a small dollop of whipped cream.

If you are cooking gluten free, always read labels to make sure each recipe ingredient is gluten free. Products and ingredient sources can change.

orange-chocolate-date cookies

prep time: 20 Minutes • **start to finish:** 2 Hours • **3 dozen cookies**

- **2** rolls Pillsbury refrigerated sugar cookies
- **¼** cup unsweetened baking cocoa
- **¼** cup orange marmalade
- **1** teaspoon orange-flavored liqueur or orange-flavored extract
- **1** teaspoon vanilla
- **1** tablespoon water
- **1** package (8 oz) chopped dates
- **1** cup chopped cashews

1 Heat oven to 350°F (or 325°F for dark or nonstick cookie sheets). Spray large cookie sheets with cooking spray. Let cookie dough stand at room temperature 10 minutes to soften.

2 In large bowl, break up cookie dough. Add cocoa, marmalade, liqueur, vanilla and water; beat with electric mixer on medium speed until blended. Stir in dates and cashews until well blended. Cover; refrigerate 30 minutes for easier handling.

3 Shape dough into 36 (1¾-inch) balls. Bake 11 to 18 minutes or until puffed and edges are set. Do not overbake. Cool on cookie sheets 2 minutes; remove to cooling racks. Cool completely, about 15 minutes. Store in covered container.

1 Cookie: Calories 160; Total Fat 6g (Saturated Fat 1.5g, Trans Fat 1.5g); Cholesterol 0mg; Sodium 85mg; Total Carbohydrate 24g (Dietary Fiber 0g); Protein 1g **Exchanges:** ½ Starch, 1 Other Carbohydrate, 1 Fat **Carbohydrate Choices:** 1½

tropical almond cookie cups

prep time: 15 Minutes • **start to finish:** 1 Hour 10 Minutes • **1 dozen cookies**

1 roll Pillsbury refrigerated sugar cookies

Generous ½ cup whole almonds, ground to ⅔ cup

2 containers (6 oz each) vanilla Greek yogurt

1 cup fresh fruit (chopped kiwifruit, pineapple or mango)

1 Heat oven to 350°F. Spray 12 regular-size muffin cups with cooking spray.

2 In medium bowl, break up cookie dough. Stir or knead in almonds. Roll dough into 12 balls. Place in muffin cups. Bake 15 to 20 minutes or until golden brown.

3 Using end of wooden spoon, carefully press into center of each baked cookie to make indentation. Bake 3 to 5 minutes longer or until set. Cool completely, about 30 minutes. Remove cookie cups from pan.

4 Spoon about 2 tablespoons yogurt into each cookie cup. Top with fresh fruit.

1 Cookie: Calories 220; Total Fat 9g (Saturated Fat 2g, Trans Fat 2g); Cholesterol 5mg; Sodium 140mg; Total Carbohydrate 30g (Dietary Fiber 1g); Protein 4g **Exchanges:** 1½ Starch, ½ Other Carbohydrate, 1½ Fat **Carbohydrate Choices:** 2

Easy Success Tips

Sprinkle toasted almonds on top of the fruit for a crunchy treat.

Dress it up by drizzling with dark or white chocolate.

lemon-blueberry cheesecake cookies

prep time: 40 Minutes • start to finish: 1 Hour 30 Minutes • 2 dozen cookies

2 oz cream cheese

1 roll Pillsbury refrigerated sugar cookies

¼ cup all-purpose flour

2 tablespoons grated lemon peel

1 cup blueberries

Powdered sugar

1 Place cream cheese in freezer until firm but not solid, about 25 minutes. Heat oven to 350°F.

2 In large bowl, break up cookie dough. Stir or knead in flour and lemon peel until well blended.

3 Cut firm cream cheese into 72 (¼-inch) cubes.

4 Shape 1 level measuring tablespoonful of dough into ball. Make 3 indentations with end of wooden spoon. Fill each indentation with 1 cube cream cheese. Wrap dough around cream cheese to completely enclose, and shape into ball. Place balls 2 inches apart on ungreased cookie sheet. Press 4 or 5 blueberries into each ball of dough.

5 Bake 10 to 14 minutes or until edges are light golden brown. Cool 5 minutes; remove from cookie sheet to cooling rack. Cool completely. Sprinkle with powdered sugar.

1 Cookie: Calories 100; Total Fat 4g (Saturated Fat 1.5g, Trans Fat 1g); Cholesterol 0mg; Sodium 70mg; Total Carbohydrate 14g (Dietary Fiber 0g); Protein 1g **Exchanges:** 1 Other Carbohydrate, 1 Fat **Carbohydrate Choices:** 1

Easy Success Tips

Freezing the cream cheese makes it easier to cut into tiny pieces and place in the dough.

Fresh blueberries are best in this recipe, but frozen blueberries can be used in a pinch.

malted milk ball–peanut butter cream squares

prep time: 20 Minutes • **start to finish:** 2 Hours 50 Minutes • 24 squares

1 roll Pillsbury™ refrigerated peanut butter cookies

1 cup whipping cream

1 container vanilla creamy ready-to-spread frosting

2 cups creamy peanut butter

1 jar (7 oz) marshmallow creme

2 cups coarsely chopped malted milk balls

½ cup chocolate-flavor syrup

1 Heat oven to 350°F. Spray 13x9-inch pan with cooking spray. Break up cookie dough, and press evenly in bottom of pan. Bake 15 to 20 minutes or until golden brown. Cool completely, about 30 minutes.

2 In medium bowl, beat whipping cream with electric mixer on high speed until soft peaks form.

3 In large bowl, beat frosting and peanut butter with electric mixer on medium speed until well blended. Carefully fold whipped cream, marshmallow creme and 1½ cups of the malted milk balls into peanut butter mixture. Spoon and spread mixture over cooled cookie crust. Refrigerate about 2 hours or until cream layer is set. Cut into 6 rows by 4 rows.

4 To serve, place cream squares on dessert plates. Drizzle each with 1 teaspoon of the chocolate syrup. Sprinkle with remaining chopped malted milk balls. Store covered in refrigerator.

1 Square: Calories 410; Total Fat 23g (Saturated Fat 7g, Trans Fat 2g); Cholesterol 15mg; Sodium 260mg; Total Carbohydrate 44g (Dietary Fiber 1g); Protein 7g **Exchanges:** 2 Starch, 1 Other Carbohydrate, 4½ Fat **Carbohydrate Choices:** 3

cup o' joe chocolate cookies

prep time: 40 Minutes • **start to finish:** 1 Hour 15 Minutes • 2½ dozen cookies

1 roll Pillsbury refrigerated sugar cookies

⅓ cup unsweetened baking cocoa

4½ teaspoons instant espresso coffee powder or granules

¼ cup whipping cream

⅓ cup miniature semisweet chocolate chips

1 Let cookie dough stand at room temperature 10 minutes to soften. Meanwhile, heat oven to 350°F.

2 In large bowl, mix cocoa, espresso powder and whipping cream with wooden spoon until well blended. Crumble cookie dough into cocoa mixture; stir until well blended.

3 Shape dough into 30 balls. On ungreased cookie sheets, place balls 2 inches apart. Using bottom of drinking glass, flatten each ball into 1½-inch round. Press thumb into center of each round to make indentation. Fill each indentation with ½ teaspoon of the chocolate chips.

4 Bake 9 to 13 minutes or until edges are set. Cool 2 minutes; remove from cookie sheets to cooling racks. Cool completely, about 20 minutes.

1 Cookie: Calories 90; Total Fat 4g (Saturated Fat 1.5g, Trans Fat 1g); Cholesterol 0mg; Sodium 50mg; Total Carbohydrate 12g (Dietary Fiber 0g); Protein 1g **Exchanges:** 1 Other Carbohydrate, 1 Fat **Carbohydrate Choices:** 1

candied hazelnut truffle bars

prep time: 30 Minutes • **start to finish:** 2 Hours • 24 bars

1 roll Pillsbury refrigerated sugar cookies

6 tablespoons plus 1½ teaspoons sugar

1 cup chopped hazelnuts

2 tablespoons butter

1 container (8 oz) mascarpone cheese

¾ cup chocolate-flavored hazelnut spread

¼ teaspoon kosher (coarse) salt

1 Heat oven to 350°F. Spray 13x9-inch pan with cooking spray. Let cookie dough stand at room temperature 10 minutes to soften. Break up cookie dough and press in pan; sprinkle with 1½ teaspoons of the sugar.

2 Bake 15 to 18 minutes or until edges are light golden brown. Remove from oven; place on cooling rack. Run knife around edge to loosen. Cool completely, about 40 minutes.

3 Meanwhile, in 12-inch skillet, mix hazelnuts, remaining 6 tablespoons of the sugar and the butter. Cook over medium heat 5 to 7 minutes, stirring until nuts are toasted and sugarcoated. Remove from skillet; set aside.

4 In medium bowl, mix mascarpone cheese and hazelnut spread until well blended. Spread over cooled cookie crust. Top with sugared hazelnuts. Sprinkle with salt; press in lightly. Refrigerate 30 minutes. Cut into 6 rows by 4 rows. Store covered in refrigerator.

1 Bar: Calories 230; Total Fat 15g (Saturated Fat 5g, Trans Fat 1g); Cholesterol 15mg; Sodium 110mg; Total Carbohydrate 21g (Dietary Fiber 0g); Protein 2g **Exchanges:** ½ Starch, 1 Other Carbohydrate, 3 Fat **Carbohydrate Choices:** 1½

24-karat cookie bars

prep time: **15 Minutes** • start to finish: **2 Hours** • **24 bars**

1 **package Pillsbury Ready to Bake! refrigerated sugar cookies**

1 **bag (11.8 oz) frozen honey Dijon carrots**

2 **teaspoons ground cinnamon**

2 **eggs**

¼ **cup self-rising flour**

1 **cup coconut pecan creamy ready-to-spread frosting**

2 **tablespoons coarse white sparkling sugar**

1 Heat oven to 350°F. Arrange cookie dough rounds evenly in ungreased 13x9-inch pan. Bake 15 to 20 minutes or until edges are light golden brown. Remove from oven; cool 5 minutes.

2 Meanwhile, microwave frozen carrots as directed on bag. Cool 5 minutes. In large food processor, place cooked carrots. Cover; process, using quick on-and-off motions until finely chopped, scraping sides occasionally. Add cinnamon, eggs, flour and frosting. Cover; process using quick on-and-off motions until mixture is blended.

3 Pour mixture evenly over partially baked crust. Bake 25 to 30 minutes longer or until top looks dry and center springs back when lightly touched.

4 Sprinkle with sugar. Let stand 5 minutes. Run knife around edges of pan to loosen; cut into 6 rows by 4 rows. Cool completely, about 45 minutes. Serve at room temperature. Store covered in refrigerator.

1 Bar: Calories 170; Total Fat 8g (Saturated Fat 2.5g, Trans Fat 0.5g); Cholesterol 15mg; Sodium 115mg; Total Carbohydrate 21g (Dietary Fiber 0g); Protein 1g **Exchanges:** ½ Starch, 1 Other Carbohydrate, 1½ Fat **Carbohydrate Choices:** 1½

chocolate and pb marshmallow squares

prep time: 20 Minutes • **start to finish:** 50 Minutes • 16 squares

1   can Pillsbury™ Grands!™ Big & Buttery refrigerated crescent dinner rolls (8 rolls)

¾   cup creamy peanut butter

3   tablespoons packed brown sugar

1¾   cups miniature marshmallows

2   bars (1.55 oz each) milk chocolate candy, broken into small pieces

1   egg white, beaten

2   tablespoons granulated sugar

1 Heat oven to 375°F. Line cookie sheet with cooking parchment paper. Unroll dough; separate into 2 rectangles. Place 1 rectangle on cookie sheet; press perforations to seal.

2 In small bowl, mix peanut butter and brown sugar. Spread over dough to within ¼ inch of edges. Press marshmallows into peanut butter mixture; top with candy bars and remaining dough rectangle. Press edges and perforations to seal. Brush top with egg white; sprinkle with granulated sugar.

3 Bake 15 to 20 minutes or until deep golden brown. Cool 10 minutes. Serve warm or cool.

1 Square: Calories 220; Total Fat 11g (Saturated Fat 4g, Trans Fat 0g); Cholesterol 0mg; Sodium 230mg; Total Carbohydrate 24g (Dietary Fiber 1g); Protein 4g **Exchanges:** 1½ Other Carbohydrate, ½ High-Fat Meat, 1½ Fat **Carbohydrate Choices:** 1½

so-easy lemon bars

prep time: 15 Minutes • start to finish: 1 Hour 35 Minutes • 36 bars

1 roll Pillsbury refrigerated sugar cookies

4 eggs, slightly beaten

1½ cups granulated sugar

2 tablespoons all-purpose flour

2 tablespoons butter or margarine, softened

2 tablespoons grated lemon peel (2 medium)

⅓ cup fresh lemon juice (2 medium)

1 to 2 tablespoons powdered sugar

1 Heat oven to 350°F. In ungreased 13x9-inch pan, break up cookie dough. With floured fingers, press dough evenly in bottom of pan to form crust. Bake 15 to 20 minutes or until light golden brown.

2 In large bowl, beat eggs with whisk or fork until well blended. Beat in granulated sugar, flour and butter until well blended. Stir in lemon peel and lemon juice. Pour mixture over warm crust.

3 Bake 20 to 30 minutes longer or until edges are light golden brown. Cool completely, about 30 minutes. Sprinkle with powdered sugar. With knife dipped in hot water, cut into 6 rows by 6 rows.

1 Bar: Calories 110; Total Fat 4g (Saturated Fat 1.5g, Trans Fat 0.5g); Cholesterol 30mg; Sodium 45mg; Total Carbohydrate 17g (Dietary Fiber 0g); Protein 1g **Exchanges:** 1 Other Carbohydrate, 1 Fat **Carbohydrate Choices:** 1

lemon-blueberry pretzel cheesecake squares

prep time: 20 Minutes • **start to finish:** 3 Hours 30 Minutes • 24 squares

1 roll Pillsbury refrigerated sugar cookies

1½ cups coarsely crushed pretzels

1 pint (2 cups) blueberries

3 packages (8 oz each) cream cheese, softened

½ cup sugar

2 teaspoons vanilla

2 tablespoons grated lemon peel

3 eggs

Additional 2 cups blueberries for garnish, if desired

1 Heat oven to 350°F. Spray 13x9-inch pan with cooking spray.

2 In medium bowl, break up cookie dough. Stir or knead in 1 cup of the pretzel crumbs. Press cookie dough evenly in bottom of pan. (If dough is sticky, use floured fingers.) Bake 5 minutes. Arrange 2 cups blueberries evenly on crust.

3 In medium bowl, beat cream cheese, sugar, vanilla and lemon peel with electric mixer on medium-high speed about 1 minute or until well blended. Add eggs; beat about 2 minutes or until well blended and creamy. Gently spoon evenly over blueberries.

4 Bake 27 to 33 minutes or until set at least 2 inches from edge of pan but center still jiggles slightly when moved (it will become firm during refrigeration). Cool 1 hour. Refrigerate about 1½ hours or until chilled and firm. Cut into 8 rows by 3 rows.

5 Spoon 1 teaspoon of the remaining pretzel crumbs and a few blueberries over each serving.

1 Square: Calories 230; Total Fat 14g (Saturated Fat 7g, Trans Fat 1.5g); Cholesterol 55mg; Sodium 210mg; Total Carbohydrate 22g (Dietary Fiber 0g); Protein 3g **Exchanges:** 1½ Other Carbohydrate, ½ High-Fat Meat, 2 Fat **Carbohydrate Choices:** 1½

Easy Success Tips

Line pan with foil to make cutting bars easier and cleanup a snap.

To quickly soften cream cheese, remove from wrapper and place on microwavable plate. Microwave uncovered on Medium (50%) 30 seconds; let stand 1 to 2 minutes.

gluten-free chocolate chip cheesecake bars

prep time: **15 Minutes** • start to finish: **2 Hours 15 Minutes** • **16 bars**

1 **container Pillsbury Gluten Free refrigerated chocolate chip cookie dough**

2 **packages (8 oz each) gluten-free cream cheese, softened**

½ **cup sugar**

1 **teaspoon gluten-free vanilla**

2 **eggs**

Gluten-free chocolate-flavor syrup, hot fudge or strawberry topping, if desired

1 Heat oven to 350°F. Grease or spray 9-inch square pan. Spoon cookie dough into bottom only of pan; press evenly in bottom of pan.

2 Bake 15 minutes. Meanwhile, in medium bowl, beat cream cheese and sugar with electric mixer on low speed about 30 seconds or until blended. Beat in vanilla and eggs, one at a time. Spread filling evenly over partially baked crust.

3 Bake 28 to 32 minutes longer or until puffed and center is just set. Cool 30 minutes on cooling rack. Refrigerate until cold, at least 1 hour. Cut into 4 rows by 4 rows. Drizzle each serving with chocolate syrup. Store covered in refrigerator.

1 Bar: Calories 240; Total Fat 15g (Saturated Fat 8g, Trans Fat 0g); Cholesterol 65mg; Sodium 190mg; Total Carbohydrate 23g (Dietary Fiber 0g); Protein 3g **Exchanges:** 1 Starch, ½ Other Carbohydrate, 3 Fat **Carbohydrate Choices:** 1½

Easy Success Tips

Delight your guests, and make these bars extra fancy. First, drizzle chocolate syrup on the dessert plate in any pattern you desire. Place bar over syrup, and drizzle a bit more on top.

If you are cooking gluten free, always read labels to make sure each recipe ingredient is gluten free. Products and ingredient sources can change.

layered salted caramel bars

prep time: 15 Minutes • **start to finish:** 1 Hour • 12 bars

⅓ cup butter, melted

½ cup packed brown sugar

1 tablespoon corn syrup

½ teaspoon salt

½ cup chopped pecans

½ cup granulated sugar

1 tablespoon ground cinnamon

3 cans (8 oz each) Pillsbury Crescent Recipe Creations refrigerated seamless dough sheet

¼ cup butter, melted

1 Heat oven to 350°F. In small bowl, mix ⅓ cup melted butter, the brown sugar, corn syrup and salt. Spread evenly in ungreased 13x9-inch pan. Sprinkle with pecans.

2 In small bowl, mix granulated sugar and cinnamon. Unroll one of the dough sheets. Press into 13x9-inch rectangle. Place in pan. Brush with some of the ¼ cup melted butter, and sprinkle with some of the cinnamon-sugar. Repeat with remaining dough sheets, ¼ cup melted butter and the cinnamon-sugar, ending with cinnamon-sugar.

3 Cover with foil. Bake 20 minutes. Remove foil; bake 25 to 30 minutes longer or until deep golden brown. Immediately turn pan upside down onto heatproof tray or serving plate. Let stand 1 minute so caramel will drizzle over bars; remove pan. Cut into 4 rows by 3 rows.

1 Bar: Calories 380; Total Fat 21g (Saturated Fat 10g, Trans Fat 0g); Cholesterol 25mg; Sodium 630mg; Total Carbohydrate 44g (Dietary Fiber 0g); Protein 3g **Exchanges:** 1½ Starch, 1½ Other Carbohydrate, 4 Fat **Carbohydrate Choices:** 3

Easy Success Tips

If you can't find Pillsbury Crescent Recipe Creations refrigerated seamless dough sheets, you can substitute Pillsbury refrigerated crescent dinner rolls. Just be sure to firmly press perforations to seal.

These bars are best served straight from the oven while the caramel is still warm.

crunchy monkey bars

prep time: 15 Minutes • **start to finish:** 2 Hours 20 Minutes • 32 bars

1 roll (16.5 oz) Pillsbury refrigerated chocolate chip cookies

1 roll Pillsbury refrigerated peanut butter cookies

1 cup mashed peeled bananas (2 medium)

1 cup chocolate-flavored hazelnut spread

1 cup crushed dried banana chips

1 Heat oven to 375°F. Spray 15x10x1-inch pan with cooking spray. Let cookie dough stand at room temperature 10 minutes to soften. In large bowl, break up both rolls of cookie dough; mix with wooden spoon or knead with hands. Stir in mashed bananas; mix well. Spread in pan.

2 Bake 18 to 22 minutes or until top is golden brown and toothpick inserted in center comes out clean. Remove from oven; immediately spoon chocolate hazelnut spread over top. Let stand 20 seconds to soften; spread evenly over crust. Top with banana chips; cool 30 minutes. Refrigerate at least 1 hour before serving. Cut into 8 rows by 4 rows. Store covered.

1 Bar: Calories 160; Total Fat 8g (Saturated Fat 2.5g, Trans Fat 1.5g); Cholesterol 0mg; Sodium 115mg; Total Carbohydrate 20g (Dietary Fiber 0g); Protein 1g **Exchanges:** ½ Starch, 1 Other Carbohydrate, 1½ Fat **Carbohydrate Choices:** 1

gluten-free chocolate chip turtle bars

prep time: 15 Minutes • **start to finish:** 2 Hours • 24 bars

Cookie Base

1 container Pillsbury Gluten Free refrigerated chocolate chip cookie dough

¾ cup chopped pecans

Filling

30 caramels, unwrapped

¼ cup whipping cream

Topping

1½ cups semisweet chocolate chips

¼ cup plus 3 tablespoons whipping cream

¼ cup chopped pecans

1 Heat oven to 350°F. Grease or spray 9-inch square pan. Spoon cookie dough in pan; press evenly in bottom of pan. Sprinkle with ¾ cup pecans; gently press pecans into dough. Bake 15 minutes. Cool 30 minutes.

2 Meanwhile, in medium microwavable bowl, microwave filling ingredients uncovered on High 2 to 3 minutes, stirring twice, until caramels are melted. Stir until smooth. Spread over cooled cookie base. Refrigerate 15 minutes.

3 In another medium microwavable bowl, microwave chocolate chips and ¼ cup plus 3 tablespoons whipping cream uncovered on High 1 to 2 minutes, stirring every 30 seconds, until chocolate is smooth. Pour over filling. Sprinkle with ¼ cup pecans. Refrigerate until set, 1 to 2 hours. Cut into 6 rows by 4 rows. Store covered in refrigerator.

1 Bar: Calories 240; Total Fat 13g (Saturated Fat 5g, Trans Fat 0g); Cholesterol 15mg; Sodium 100mg; Total Carbohydrate 27g (Dietary Fiber 1g); Protein 2g **Exchanges:** ½ Starch, 1½ Other Carbohydrate, 2½ Fat **Carbohydrate Choices:** 2

Easy Success Tips

For a special occasion when you want smaller treats, cut into 6 rows by 6 rows. Place cut bars in decorative mini foil baking cups. Visit a cake decorating supply store for the best selection of cups.

If you are cooking gluten free, always read labels to make sure each recipe ingredient is gluten free. Products and ingredient sources can change.

caramel cashew bars

prep time: 20 Minutes • start to finish: 1 Hour 20 Minutes • 36 bars

- 1 roll (16.5 oz) Pillsbury refrigerated chocolate chip cookies
- 1 bag (11.5 oz) milk chocolate chips (2 cups)
- 1 container (18 oz) caramel apple dip (1½ cups)
- 3 cups crisp rice cereal
- 1¼ cups cashew halves and pieces

1 Heat oven to 350°F. In ungreased 13x9-inch pan, break up cookie dough. With floured fingers, press dough evenly in bottom of pan to form crust.

2 Bake 15 to 18 minutes or until light golden brown. Cool 15 minutes.

3 Meanwhile, in 3- to 4-quart saucepan, cook 1 cup of the chocolate chips and 1 cup of the dip over medium heat, stirring constantly, until melted and smooth. Remove from heat. Stir in cereal and cashews.

4 Spread cereal mixture over crust. In 1-quart saucepan, heat remaining chocolate chips and dip over medium heat, stirring constantly, until melted and smooth. Spread over cereal mixture. Refrigerate until chocolate mixture is set, about 30 minutes. Cut into 6 by 6 rows.

1 Bar: Calories 180; Total Fat 7g (Saturated Fat 2.5g, Trans Fat 0g); Cholesterol 0mg; Sodium 120mg; Total Carbohydrate 26g (Dietary Fiber 0g); Protein 2g **Exchanges:** ½ Starch, 1 Other Carbohydrate, 1½ Fat **Carbohydrate Choices:** 2

chocolate–peanut butter pretzel bars

prep time: 25 Minutes • **start to finish:** 2 Hours 35 Minutes • 24 bars

1 package Pillsbury Ready to Bake! refrigerated sugar cookies

1¾ cups pretzels

2 tablespoons butter flavor shortening

1 can (14 oz) sweetened condensed milk (not evaporated)

¾ cup creamy peanut butter

½ cup chocolate-flavored hazelnut spread

¼ cup caramel topping

1 Heat oven to 350°F. Spray 13x9-inch pan with cooking spray. Let cookie dough stand at room temperature 10 minutes to soften.

2 Finely chop 1 cup of the pretzels; place in large bowl. Add cookie dough and shortening. Beat with electric mixer on low speed until well mixed. Press dough evenly in pan. Bake 14 to 18 minutes or until crust is light golden brown. Cool 10 minutes.

3 Meanwhile, in 2-quart heavy saucepan, heat condensed milk over medium heat 5 to 8 minutes, stirring constantly, until hot and mixture is thin. Remove from heat. Stir in peanut butter and chocolate hazelnut spread until well blended. Spread over baked crust. Coarsely chop remaining ¾ cup pretzels; sprinkle on top. Bake 15 to 20 minutes longer or until edges are golden brown. Cool completely, about 1½ hours. Drizzle with caramel topping. Cut into 6 rows by 4 rows. Store covered.

1 Bar: Calories 220; Total Fat 11g (Saturated Fat 3.5g, Trans Fat 0g); Cholesterol 5mg; Sodium 180mg; Total Carbohydrate 28g (Dietary Fiber 0g); Protein 4g **Exchanges:** 1½ Starch, ½ Other Carbohydrate, 2 Fat **Carbohydrate Choices:** 2

Easy Success Tip

Instead of chopping the pretzels, place pretzels in large resealable food-storage plastic bag. Seal bag; with rolling pin, coarsely crush pretzels. Remove ¾ cup. Seal bag and finely crush remaining pretzels in bag.

gluten-free rocky road bars

prep time: **10 Minutes** • start to finish: **2 Hours 35 Minutes** • **30 bars**

1 **container Pillsbury Gluten Free refrigerated chocolate chip cookie dough**

2 **cups semisweet chocolate chips**

½ **cup coarsely chopped peanuts**

3 **cups miniature marshmallows**

1 Heat oven to 350°F. Grease or spray 13x9-inch pan. Spoon cookie dough in bottom only of pan; press evenly in bottom of pan.

2 Bake 15 minutes. Immediately sprinkle chocolate chips over crust. Let stand 3 to 5 minutes or until chocolate begins to melt. Gently spread chocolate evenly over crust.

3 Set oven control to broil. Sprinkle peanuts and marshmallows over melted chocolate. Broil with top 5 to 6 inches from heat 20 to 30 seconds or until marshmallows are toasted. (Watch closely; marshmallows will brown quickly.) Cool 30 to 45 minutes to serve warm, or cool completely, about 2 hours. Cut into 6 rows by 5 rows, using sharp knife sprayed with cooking spray. Store tightly covered.

1 Bar: Calories 150; Total Fat 7g (Saturated Fat 3g, Trans Fat 0g); Cholesterol 5mg; Sodium 55mg; Total Carbohydrate 20g (Dietary Fiber 1g); Protein 1g **Exchanges:** ½ Starch, 1 Other Carbohydrate, 1½ Fat **Carbohydrate Choices:** 1

Easy Success Tips

Dairy free? We tested these bars with dairy-free chocolate chips and had excellent results!

If you are cooking gluten free, always read labels to make sure each recipe ingredient is gluten free. Products and ingredient sources can change.

gluten-free chocolate chip cookie layer bars

prep time: **10 Minutes** • start to finish: **2 Hours 55 Minutes** • **36 bars**

1 **container Pillsbury Gluten Free refrigerated chocolate chip cookie dough**

1 **can (14 oz) sweetened condensed milk (not evaporated)**

1 **bag (12 oz) white vanilla baking chips (2 cups)**

1 **cup flaked coconut**

1 **cup chopped walnuts**

1 Heat oven to 350°F. Grease or spray 13x9-inch pan. Spoon cookie dough in pan; press evenly in bottom of pan.

2 Bake 15 minutes. Drizzle condensed milk evenly over partially baked crust. Sprinkle with remaining ingredients.

3 Bake 25 to 30 minutes longer or until golden brown. Cool completely, about 2 hours. Cut into 6 rows by 6 rows.

1 Bar: Calories 170; Total Fat 9g (Saturated Fat 4.5g, Trans Fat 0g); Cholesterol 10mg; Sodium 80mg; Total Carbohydrate 20g (Dietary Fiber 0g); Protein 2g **Exchanges:** 1 Starch, ½ Other Carbohydrate, 1½ Fat **Carbohydrate Choices:** 1

Easy Success Tips

If you crave some extra chocolate, substitute 1 cup milk chocolate or semisweet chocolate chips for 1 cup vanilla baking chips.

If you are cooking gluten free, always read labels to make sure each recipe ingredient is gluten free. Products and ingredient sources can change.

Metric Conversion Guide

VOLUME

U.S. Units	Canadian Metric	Australian Metric
¼ teaspoon	1 mL	1 ml
½ teaspoon	2 mL	2 ml
1 teaspoon	5 mL	5 ml
1 tablespoon	15 mL	20 ml
¼ cup	50 mL	60 ml
⅓ cup	75 mL	80 ml
½ cup	125 mL	125 ml
⅔ cup	150 mL	170 ml
¾ cup	175 mL	190 ml
1 cup	250 mL	250 ml
1 quart	1 liter	1 liter
1½ quarts	1.5 liters	1.5 liters
2 quarts	2 liters	2 liters
2½ quarts	2.5 liters	2.5 liters
3 quarts	3 liters	3 liters
4 quarts	4 liters	4 liters

WEIGHT

U.S. Units	Canadian Metric	Australian Metric
1 ounce	30 grams	30 grams
2 ounces	55 grams	60 grams
3 ounces	85 grams	90 grams
4 ounces (¼ pound)	115 grams	125 grams
8 ounces (½ pound)	225 grams	225 grams
16 ounces (1 pound)	455 grams	500 grams
1 pound	455 grams	0.5 kilogram

MEASUREMENTS

Inches	Centimeters
1	2.5
2	5.0
3	7.5
4	10.0
5	12.5
6	15.0
7	17.5
8	20.5
9	23.0
10	25.5
11	28.0
12	30.5
13	33.0

TEMPERATURES

Fahrenheit	Celsius
32°	0°
212°	100°
250°	120°
275°	140°
300°	150°
325°	160°
350°	180°
375°	190°
400°	200°
425°	220°
450°	230°
475°	240°
500°	260°

Note: The recipes in this cookbook have not been developed or tested using metric measures. When converting recipes to metric, some variations in quality may be noted.

index

Page numbers in *italics* indicate illustrations

Recipe Testing and Calculating Nutrition Information

Recipe Testing:

- Large eggs and 2% milk were used unless otherwise indicated.

- Fat-free, low-fat, low-sodium or lite products were not used unless indicated.

- No nonstick cookware and bakeware were used unless otherwise indicated. No dark-colored, black or insulated bakeware was used.

- When a pan is specified, a metal pan was used; a baking dish or pie plate means ovenproof glass was used.

- An electric hand mixer was used for mixing only when mixer speeds are specified.

Calculating Nutrition:

- The first ingredient was used wherever a choice is given, such as ⅓ cup sour cream or plain yogurt.

- The first amount was used wherever a range is given, such as 3- to 3 ½-pound whole chicken.

- The first serving number was used wherever a range is given, such as 4 to 6 servings.

- "If desired" ingredients were not included.

- Only the amount of a marinade or frying oil that is absorbed was included.